Arts Education Based on Dewey's Occupation

Artistic Construction Activity

KOJIMA Ritsuko

Hokuju Shuppan

KOJIMA Ritsuko,
Arts Education Based on Dewey's Occupation:
Artistic Construction Activity
2023.10.1
ISBN978-4-7793-0721-8
©2023, KOJIMA Ritsuko, printed in Japan
This edition is published by Hokuju Shuppan Co.Ltd.,
Nakameguro 1-2-6 Meguro-ku Tokyo-to Japan,
Tel. +81-3-3715-1525
URL : http://www.hokuju.jp

Preface

My consistent concern has been how to change the fixed notion in society that regards art as something isolated and reserved for the "cultured" few. John Dewey's *Art as Experience*, a theory of art that sees the origin of art as a life-sustaining impulse, was precisely the answer to my concern. Art lies not within the possession of portraits of musicians like Bach and Beethoven in the school music rooms; rather, art is something that every human being possesses as an impulse to create from the moment they are born into the world. Based on Dewey's theory of occupation, which is rooted in everyday experience, I formulated the idea of "artistic construction activity" as an educational method to continuously develop everyday experience, starting from impulse, into artistic experience. This serves as the link between Dewey's theories of education and art.

Just as Dewey recognized the significance of occupation in human development amidst the social transformation caused by the Industrial Revolution in the 18th and 19th centuries, we can recognize the significance of artistic construction activity in human development amidst the social transformation caused by AI in the 21st century. It is my hope that the concept of artistic construction activity proposed in this book will be critiqued and reconfigured by those who follow.

I would like to express my appreciation for the valuable ideas and suggestions I received from the following individuals in the preparation of this manuscript.

Professor Emeritus of Nagoya University Hibi, Yutaka; Professor Emeritus of Naruto University of Education Nishizono, Yoshinobu; Professor Emeritus of Ochanomizu University Tokumaru, Yoshihiko; members of the Japan Dewey Society; members of the Kansai Music Education Practice and Research Association.

Note: This is an abridged English version of "*Artistic Construction Activity based on Dewey's Concept of Occupation*" [Dewey no okyupe-shon gainen ni motozuku geijututeki kosei katudo] published by Kazama-shobo, Tokyo, 2021.

Contents

preface ·· 3

Introduction: The Age of Artificial Intelligence and Artistic Education ·········· 7

1   The Concept of Occupation as an Educational Method ···················· 13
An overview of occupation   13
The concept of occupation as an educational method   21

2   The Connection Between Artistic Experience and Occupation ············· 38
Essence, methodological principles, and structure of artistic experience   38
Continuity from occupations to artistic experience   56

3   A Theory of Artistic Construction Activity Based on the Concept of Occupation ·········· 65
Essence and methodological principles of artistic construction activity   65
Structure of artistic construction activity   70

4   An Activity Model and Practice of Artistic Construction Activity ·········· 90
An activity model for artistic construction activity   90
Example of activity model in practice   103

5   Typical Artistic Construction Activities ···························· 116
Music-making   116
Song-writing   121
Instrument-making   125
Graphic score-making   127

6

Conclusion: The Significance and Prospects of Artistic Construction Activity · 134

Significance and challenges of artistic construction activity in school education

134

Prospects for artistic construction activity in the age of AI   143

REFERENCES ·· 148

ABOUT THE AUTHOR ·· 150

Introduction
The Age of Artificial Intelligence and
Artistic Education

The 21st century will be known as the age of Artificial Intelligence (AI). The emergence of AI has caused enormous social changes on a scale unseen since the Industrial Revolution. Amid these changes, direct experiences with the real world are necessary to ensure that mankind does not become subservient to AI and that we are able to retain our humanity. Direct experience here refers to experiences that use the body's sensory organs to directly perceive the world rather than indirect experiences, which are mediated through signs and symbols. This kind of experience allows us to perceive the "qualities" of the real world (e.g., the fragrance of freshly toasted bread and the reflection of morning dew on the grass). The perception of these qualities of the real world helps us maintain the self-awareness that we are alive, right here at this moment. These qualities ensure that we retain our humanlike qualities (Reese, 2018).

As Douglas N. Sloan pointed out, an effective way to train our sensory organs to be more sensitive toward real-world qualities is through artistic education (Sloan, 1983, pp. 218-221). However, if we were to ask ourselves if the artistic education taking place in schools has successfully accomplished this mission thus far? The answer will have to be no.

Realities of Artistic Education in Schools

In the Japanese school system, music and art are subjects that everyone must take in the nine years of compulsory education, starting from elementary school to junior high school. This means that every child is engaged in music and art lessons on a weekly basis for this duration. Despite this, except for a few art enthusiasts, most adults lead lives that are unrelated to the arts once they have graduated from

8

school. The fact remains that such adults remove themselves from the arts, apologetic that "something like that is too profound for me" or "I am just a layperson" when a discussion about the arts arises.

The reason for this unfortunate state of affairs is the traditional mindset toward the arts, which has dominated artistic education in schools. This traditional mindset views the arts as something high-brow and distant from everyday life. As a result, when we discuss art, those of us who were educated based on this mindset think of works in a museum or music in a concert hall, and we understand art as something that is sophisticated and disconnected from daily life.

The kind of beauty pursued by the traditional mindset toward artistic education is something out of reach and far removed from schoolchildren. Further, children are expected to work hard and get as close as possible to this kind of beauty by learning the relevant knowledge and skills from those who are more advanced in the arts. Because of this, there is a tendency to produce a kind of education that is entirely dictated by prescribed standards, an education centered on skill instructions. While this kind of education might be enjoyable for a small group of children who are able to adapt, the rest of the children fail to do so and feel that they lack aptitude for the arts. They struggle to meet the objectives laid upon them and end up adopting the mindset that they are no good at the arts; this leads to them naturally distancing themselves from arts upon graduation.

Artistic Education Based on Dewey's Theory of the Arts

Instead of the traditional conceptualization of art, where it is seen as something high-brow, John Dewey proposed a new way of looking at the arts where a connection is forged between the arts and everyday experiences. In 1934, Dewey offered his new theories about art in the book *Art as Experience*. He discusses art as an act of impulse that is necessary to maintain human survival and is a continuation of everyday experience. This theory of art brought about a paradigm shift in the world of aesthetics, which previously assumed a heavenly and divine form of beauty. Unsurprisingly, Dewey's book was hardly accepted by the aesthetic world when it was first published. However, it was regarded as the most valuable work about aesthetics in the twentieth century (Jackson, 1998, pp. xi–xii).

We can say that in Dewey's aesthetic theory, which views the arts as an extension of everyday experiences, what connect the arts to these everyday experiences are the abovementioned "qualities" of the real world. Dewey argues that art work has a unique *quality* "of clarifying and concentrating meanings contained in scattered and weakened ways in the material of other experiences" (*LW*10, p.90). Art expresses the qualitative meaning behind our everyday experiences through qualitative mediums, such as sound and colors. Therefore, education grounded in Dewey's aesthetic theory, which view art as a qualitative experience, can cultivate sensitivity toward the qualitative aspects of our real world in children.

Dewey's position is that art is something connected to everyday life, and it is possible for anyone to experience art as part of their own life. This means that an education that endorses Dewey's position does not see art as a privilege exclusive only to those in the higher echelons of society but rather believes that it is possible for all children living in this world to experience art. His theories urge schools to make drastic reforms to existing methods of artistic education.

Pedagogy in the New Artistic Education

How can we realize Dewey's aesthetic theories in the context of artistic education in schools? To achieve this, a new kind of education method is required, one that is fundamentally different from existing methods that emphasize and prioritize skills such as reading the notation of music scores and other symbols. This new kind of education can draw on Dewey's concept of occupation.

This is because occupation entails extending everyday experiences into knowledge, science, cultural arts, and other kinds of specialized experiences in the context of school education. We believe that it is possible to discover a educational method for a kind of artistic education that is connected to everyday life by examining the concept of occupation from the perspective of educational methodology to see how we can extend and develop everyday experiences into specialized ones.

When we examine the concept of occupation from the perspective of educational methodology, we see that it consists of interactions between "doing" and "undergoing." It is an activity that uses the body to construct something externally. However, the crucial point is that this external construction is an expression of something within the child, whether it is an image, a thought, or a feeling. In other ways, the essential idea is that what is external and internal to us are not disjointed but remain connected. The objective is to reconstruct ourselves, both the internal and the external, through the interactions between "doing" and "undergoing." Dewey considers this reconstruction of one's internal "growth," and this is taken as the objective, or "end," of education.

An educational activity called "artistic construction activity" uses Dewey's concept of occupation as a theoretical framework. What is "artistic construction activity" ? Simply put, "artistic construction activity" is an activity where we use materials around us to construct a coherent and well-balanced piece of work while interacting with them. In the case of music, a possible "artistic construction activity" would be the act of expression where children choose the sounds they want to use on their own, manipulate them freely, and compose music using these sounds. This is different from the so-called process of "composing." The crucial difference is that the activity is not mediated through symbols, such as musical notes and solfa; children will actually experience these sounds through their sensory organs and put together a piece of music. Similar to occupation, the essential nature of an artistic construction activity is that it is an interaction between "doing" and "undergoing," and the construction of external materials through this interaction is associated with the internal realm of the child. In Japan, this form of artistic activity has been put into practice in schools from the Kansai area since the 1980s, and a considerable amount of related research has been accumulated (Kojima, 1993, and others).

Structure and Significance of This Book

However, existing studies mostly consist of fragmentary research on the practical and theoretical aspects of "artistic construction activity," and a systematic study that provides a clear overall picture has yet to be published. Therefore, this book seeks to construct a systematic theory for "artistic construction activity" and propose activity models that lie between theory and practice as clues to how the theory can be specifically implemented in education practice at school.

As a result, the book will be structured into three parts: theoretical foundation, theory, and practice. The first chapter explains Dewey's concept of occupation as pedagogy from the perspective of educational methodology (theoretical foundation). The second and third chapters seek to construct a theory for artistic construction activity by revealing the relation between artistic experience and occupation through an examination of Dewey's theories about art via the concept of occupation (theory). The fourth chapter formulates an activity model that can be used to put artistic construction activity into specific education practice and present relevant practical case studies (practice). The fifth chapter introduces four types of typical artistic construction activities that use sound as their material: music-making, song-writing, instrument-making, and graphic score-making. The last chapter discusses the significance and challenges of implementing artistic construction activity in school education and how this can potentially contribute to children living in the AI era, that is, the twenty-first century.

Generally, this book seeks to integrate Dewey's theories on education and art, proposing "artistic construction activity" as a new pedagogical method in the context of a school artistic education that is connected to everyday life. This can be significant in terms of accomplishing education reform, which transforms artistic education from one that sees art as an exclusive domain for a small number of children to one that contributes to a kind of character building that anyone can participate in. At the same time, this book is also significant from an academic perspective in the area of research on Dewey, as it seeks to bridge Dewey's theories on education and his theories on art.

Chapter

The Concept of Occupation as an Educational Method

Chapter 1 examines John Dewey's discourse on occupation and educes the concept of occupation as an educational method, which constitutes the theoretical foundation of "artistic construction activity."

An overview of occupation

When asked what occupations are, there is no easy answer. Dewey failed to systematically discuss occupations as a whole; his readers must search through *The School and Society*, along with parts of *Democracy and Education, How We Think*, and materials on the Laboratory School where occupations were put into practice. Moreover, Dewey made the definition of occupation more difficult to arrive at in these texts by referring to it in varying terms such as "active occupation" and "constructive occupation" and using similar phrases such as "constructive work" and "manual training" in contexts related to occupations.[1]

First, therefore, this section presents an overview of what "occupation" means based on the definitions provided by Dewey.

What are occupations?

What are occupations? Occupation in Dewey's terms referred to a mode of activity for children introduced at the Laboratory School of the University of Chicago (henceforth, the Laboratory School), the establishment and management of which

Dewey was involved in at the end of the 19th century. Dewey explained the term as follows.

> By occupation I mean a mode of activity on the part of the child, which reproduces, or runs parallel to, some form of work carried on in social life. In the University Elementary School these occupations are represented by the shop work with wood and tools, cooking, sewing, and the textile work. (*MW*1: 92)

This quotation discusses the external appearance of occupational activities. Dewey referred to occupations as activities in which children actually reproduce basic work or similar tasks required for life in society, such as cooking, sewing, and wood-work, in the societal microcosm of the school.

The idea of introducing cooking, sewing, woodwork, and so on, into schools was not originally conceived by Dewey. This idea had already been introduced at some urban schools in the US since the 1850s, as part of the trend away from traditional book learning and toward child-centered school education. Although he approved of the introduction of this type of work into schools, Dewey was critical of the fact that, at the time, this introduction took place for superficial reasons, simply to keep the children amused or to educate them for future trades (*MW*1: 9). The occupation Dewey had in mind was a concept concerned with the educational significance of work, distinct from work simply intended to keep the children active.

How, then, were Dewey's intended occupations different from those in practice in progressive schools of the time? Dewey described the fundamental point of occupa-tion from the psychological perspective of the child involved, not as an external mode of activity.

> The fundamental point in the psychology of an occupation is that it maintains a balance between the intellectual and the practical phases of experience. As an occu-pation, it is active or motor; it finds expression through the physical organs—the eyes, hands, etc. But it also involves continual observation of materials, and contin-ual planning and reflection, in order that the practical or executive side may be successfully carried on. (*MW*1: 92)

The fundamental point of occupation is here said to be the balance it maintains between the "intellectual phase" and the "practical phase" of experience. This point may be considered the basic principle of Dewey's original concept of occupation. It also constitutes the basic principle to understand occupation not as a mode of activity but as an educational method.

The practical phase refers to actual physical action used to accomplish something, transforming the materials worked upon; the intellectual phase refers to observing the process of the physical action on the materials, planning and executing what is to be done next, and reflecting upon the result. This means that children's external actions and internal thoughts are interrelated. Children do not have occupation simply by working with their hands to cook, but rather when the work of their hands is intertwined with the work of their minds.

In other words, the maintenance of balance between the practical phase, in which the eyes and hands are put to work in the manipulation of materials, and the intellectual phase, in which the mind works to keep the practice moving efficiently—that is, the unbroken interrelation between children's interior aspects and their external actions—is the fundamental point of occupation.

Accordingly, we may define Dewey's idea of occupation as a mode of activity reproducing the basic activities of social life, in which the practical and the intellectual phases are maintained in balance.

Background of the introduction of occupations to the Laboratory School

Why did Dewey attempt to introduce occupations into his school? The background of the introduction of occupations to the Laboratory School involved Dewey's intent to reform the teacher-centered, passive, uniform education conducted in US public schools at the time, moving toward active, child-centered education instead.

In the first place, Dewey founded the Laboratory School at the University of Chicago in 1896 to bring about a shift in the old-fashioned, traditional education then generally conducted in US public schools. Old-fashioned, traditional

16

education meant children sitting on chairs, passively listening as their teachers lectured, and learning what they heard by rote. The school placed teachers at its center; classrooms were a sea of desks and chairs for listening to the teachers speak, and children were forbidden to stand up or walk around at will and expected to behave uniformly (*MW*1: 21–23).

In response to traditional education of this kind, Dewey proposed a new educational perspective that placed children rather than teachers at the center of the school. This has been compared with the Copernican Revolution (*MW*1: 23). Upon the establishment of the Laboratory School, Dewey conceived of occupations as a method for realizing this new educational perspective in school. That is, in response to the issue of putting new, child-centered education into concrete practice, occupations were positioned as a central activity within the school curriculum.

In short, the background to the introduction of occupations was the reality of public school education at the time and how little it resembled Dewey's educational philosophy; occupations were introduced as an educational method of reform with regard to this reality. The activity content and educational significance of occupations were further developed through practical verification at the Laboratory School. Based on this point, occupations may be considered an educational method used to link Dewey's educational philosophy to educational practice.

Practice of occupations at the Laboratory School

What specific activities were used in the practice of occupations at the Laboratory School? *The Dewey School*, by Katherine Camp Mayhew and Anna Camp Edwards, teachers at the Laboratory School in its early days, is a record of the school's practice. This text clarifies to some extent the specific forms of occupation practiced at the Laboratory School.

1. Curriculum composition

Occupations were a space for undifferentiated experience before differentiation and specialization into various academic fields. At the Laboratory School, the issue of continuous development of the undifferentiated experience of occupations into the specialist experience of academics, science, culture, and the arts was addressed from the perspective of the curriculum. To this end, rather than making occupations a part of subject study, they were positioned as a central axis of the curriculum throughout the school; the compositional principle positioned reading, writing, arithmetic, and other academic subjects within the context of the expansion and development of occupational activities (*EW*5: 245).

This suggests that in curriculum composition, the significance of occupations was recognized not as an isolated single task activity but with a view to connections with specialized academic fields, science, culture, and the arts. More than the significance of occupations as a character-building discipline instilled by various tasks in daily life, Dewey is thought to have focused on their content in connection to academia, science, culture, and the arts, the cumulative result of the development of human experience, and to have positioned occupations within the curriculum.

2. Examples of occupations

What, then, was the specific practice of occupations at the Laboratory School? Because the record of practice published as *The Dewey School* is limited to excerpts, many of the connections between activities remain unclear. Here is an overview, albeit fragmentary, of examples of cooking and weaving.[2]

(1) Six-year-olds cooking

In the fall term, the group readied a plot in the schoolyard to plant their winter wheat. Next, they prepared for threshing. Methods of threshing the wheat (removing the grains from their hulls) were discussed. At first, they picked it out by hand. This was too slow, so they suggested beating it with a stick. They found that only the edge of the stick struck the ground. With some advice from their teacher, the children decided to join two sticks together.

The hulled wheat was used for an experiment. When they pounded it in a mortar and compared it with some fine white flour, the children saw that the inside of the grain was mixed with yellow particles. After considering how best to remove these yellow particles, they put the wheat through a sieve. However, some of the yellow particles still remained. At this point, the teacher advised the use of cheesecloth, which enabled the wheat to be sifted cleanly. Finally, the clean white flour with yellow particles removed was used to bake a cake.

When the group discussed grains in the classroom, they cooked cereals in the kitchen. This means that they had to learn how to measure. They had to know how many teaspoons equal one tablespoon and so on. They discovered that two halves make a cupful, just the same as three thirds or four quarters.

In the example above, the practice of cooking not only involved the act of cooking but also involved extended study such as the exploration of materials and processes. As the problem of how to make flour from wheat arose, the children came up with ways to solve the problem as well as invented and manufactured tools. This indicates the process of problem solving as a form of exploration. Furthermore, regarding life skills such as reading, writing, and arithmetic, spaces for study were deliberately built-in based on the work required.

(2) Twelve-year-olds weaving sheep wool

The children washed the dirty, oily raw wool of the sheep with soap of their own making, carded it with a comb of their own invention, and spun it on a spindle and wheel of their own construction. In the workshop, they constructed primitive looms based on Native American designs. Having made looms, they wanted to use them to create something. Shown Native American woven blankets, they created similar designs. They dyed the wool with self-mixed colors and, on their own looms, wove it into small rugs with self-designed patterns. During the process of learning primitive spinning and carding methods, sketches were made of the hands of the children as they spun wool.

The example above began with physically handling sheep wool, the raw material of clothing fabric. The children then went through the actual process of spinning the raw wool into yarn and weaving the yearn into cloth, reimagining for themselves the tools invented over time by humanity. Activities related to the arts, such as designing blanket patterns or sketching the work process, were also included.

(3) Discussion of examples

While the term "occupations" generally refers to cooking, sewing, woodwork, and other tasks, these examples involve not simply cooking or weaving but integrated explorative activities containing learning from historical/geographic, scientific, arithmetic, and artistic perspectives linked to the materials and processes used in the work. The activity process includes, as needed, crafting, drawing, experiments, discussion, field trips, research, cultivation, and so on, configuring an environment that enables the work experience to develop and expand. The children themselves mutually interact with raw materials like wheat and wool, encountering them directly through their physical senses rather than through linguistic symbols; this leads to the development of exploratory study of the problems arising during the process.

Abilities developed through occupations

What are the abilities that occupations are expected to develop in children? According to *The School and Society*, they are "social power" (the ability to mutually interact with the social environment) and "insight" (the ability to grasp the significance of these interactions). It is expected that these abilities will in turn develop the imagination.

1. Social power and insight

The purpose of occupations is not preparation for future employment but children's growth through interaction with materials as part of their environment, that is, through experience (*MW*1: 92). "Growth" refers to the reconstruction of experience as children acquire new meanings from their environment.

Occupations are expected to develop social power and insight as abilities involved in children's growth (*MW*1: 12). What is social power? Social power is the capacity to participate in the process of the give and take of experience (*MW*9: 127). The development of social power is the fulfillment of the social instinct, that is, the desire to recount one's own experience to others and to make others' experience one's own in return (*MW*1: 28). This becomes the desire to acquire language and, at the same time, concern with the social aspect of "people's activities and their mutual dependencies" (*MW*1: 98). Giving scope to the social instinct through occupations can be expected to cultivate children's social desires and their concerns with the social aspects of human activities. In short, social power is thought to refer to the ability to become interested and actively involved in society, i.e., one's environment—the willingness to exchange experiences with others and to carry out the responsibilities and duties of a member of society.

What, then, is insight? Occupations are not expected to enable children to attain the skills needed to carry out tasks but to put to work the insight capable of seeing through to the essence and the foundation of things. Insight here refers to the scientific insight applied to the natural materials and processes handled in occupations (*MW*1: 13). Occupations are expected, through the manipulation of materials, to activate the capacity for insight into the properties and processes inherent in the natural materials one is handling.

2. Development of the imagination

Dewey focused on occupations as educational materials which, through the development of social power and insight, would ultimately develop the imagination.

Imagination in Dewey's context does not refer to fairy tales or daydreams. Instead, it is the power to connect things far apart in time or space. Occupations are expected to develop the imagination as the familiar phenomena of daily life are connected to geographically and historically distant ones, and their meaning is revealed by insight, expanding the children's world (*MW*1: 38). Dewey argued that the development of imagination amounted to raising "cultured" people, who would be able to realize democracy. Dewey's "culture" as used here was distinct from the generally accepted concept of familiarity with cultural content. He considered "culture" to be the ability to develop inner growth through action and to contribute to society through that growth (*MW*1: 38). Dewey also believed that when nature and society existed in the schoolroom, and learning was conducted to reconstruct experience, the imagination would grow, and "culture shall be the democratic password"

(*MW*1: 38). Culture, he argued, would create democracy. The introduction of occupations in school would develop the imagination, endowing children with culture and thereby enabling them to create democracy; in this way, occupations would ultimately cultivate the people who would build a democratic society.

The concept of occupation as an educational method

This book addresses occupation as an educational method putting Dewey's educational philosophy into concrete practice, not as a learning activity or method of instruction. First, therefore, this part will discuss the positioning of occupation in Dewey's educational philosophy.

Next, it will clarify the essence and methodological principles of occupation as an educational method. Thereafter, the structure of occupation will be approached through its process, psychological, and social aspects.

Positioning of occupation in Dewey's educational philosophy

1. Harmony of the individual with society

The core of Dewey's educational philosophy is in the "harmony of the individual with society." Children must acquire the norms and customs of the society into which they are born to live there. However, individuals are called upon not only to master these social norms and customs as they are but also to achieve personal growth. Personal growth is what enables society to renew itself. Rather than attempting to prioritize either the individual or society, Dewey's philosophy of education addressed them as a continuous whole, raising the issue of how to create the "harmony of the individual with society."

To resolve this issue, Dewey focused on play and work in everyday life. Both play and work are activities that give scope to children's impulse to express themselves. By arranging for materials and conditions that evoke the impulse for individual expression in the normal social direction, the impulse can be directed rather than set off at random. Dewey felt that in this way, the "harmony of the individual with society" could be realized. He envisioned "the child's expressive activities in dealing with the fundamental social materials," citing the typical occupations of daily life (woodwork, sewing, cooking) as modes of activity (*EW*5: 229–230).

Dewey conceived of occupations in a social environment, with regard to social materials, as activities for self-expression through the natural force of impulse; he positioned occupations as an effective method of realizing the "harmony of the individual with society," which was the fundamental concern of his educational philosophy.

2. Connection between school and life

Dewey's intention to reform school through the principle of "connection between school and life" underlies his conception of occupation as an effective method of realizing the "harmony of the individual with society." To realize the "harmony of the individual with society" in school, Dewey presented the principle of "connection between school and life," focusing on the untapped educational potential of daily life.

According to Dewey, education to turn immature children into mature members of society once took place within everyday life. However, as civilization advanced and society became vaster and more complex, the systematic educational institutions known as schools were created, and education was consigned thereto. As a result, systematized school education was totally removed from non-systematic education in daily life, leading to various problems in school education (*MW*9: 11–12).

Thus, Dewey focused on learning through the society and culture embedded in daily life to close the gap between school and life. According to Dewey, children learn about the properties and applications of objects through doing, physically manipulating tools in the environment of life in society outside of school (*MW*9: 149). Learning of this kind draws on direct experience, taking part therein without the mediation of symbols.

By contrast, schools conduct education intended for the teaching of predetermined content with predetermined teaching materials. In this form of education, the academic content, science, culture, and arts to be taught are extracted and presented efficiently. Learning in this context is mediated through linguistic symbols. Dewey felt that education through life would become the foundation of school learning through linguistic symbols. According to Dewey, the absence of learning through direct life experience made it more difficult for children themselves to connect the meaning found through direct experience to the symbols thereof, potentially resulting in education intended only for the mastery of symbols. Hands-on learning through direct life experience thus became the foundation to construct learning through linguistic symbols in school (MW9: 241). School learning through linguistic symbols would then be applied once again to life, creating richer life experiences.

The educational methods introduced in this mode of education through life were activities that reorganized the educational significance embedded in work and play in life: in short, occupations. Dewey was trying to blend school and life by introducing a non-systematic framework of education in life to the school, the location of systematic education.

Occupations, deriving from life experience in this way, have their roots as an educational method in direct experience through the physical senses. However, they cannot be reduced to sporadic direct experiences. They must function as educational experiences containing, as their framework, continuity in the expansion of experience to indirect experience through symbols. Occupations can be positioned as an educational method for "education through life experience," thereby becoming the basis for "education through symbols."

Essence and methodological principles of occupation as an educational method

1. Essence

In its positioning as an educational method for "education through life experience," the essence of occupation is thought to lie in its nature as "direct experience." According to Dewey, direct experience is the source of the generation of meaning. In daily life, children use their bodies and senses to act. When their hands, eyes, and ears are used for a purpose, the qualities of the object they perceive take on meaning (*MW*9: 149). To keep "education through symbols" from becoming simply the transmission of symbols and to enable learning with a sense of reality, direct experience must be employed to accumulate sufficient "realization of sense" (*MW*9: 241). This accumulation of the realization of sense is gained through play and active work, that is, occupation. Dewey believed that a sense of reality could be regained in school education when children realized the meaning of the world around them.

Based on the above considerations, we may regard the essence of occupation as an educational method to lie in "direct experience as life experience," and we may regard its significance to be "the realization of sense through direct experience."

2. Methodological principles

What, then, are the methodological principles that enable "the realization of sense through direct experience"?

In psychological terms, Dewey considered occupations to be a form of individual self-expression. However, harmony between the individual and society requires not random expression of the self but self-expression "in such a way as to realize social ends" (*EW*5: 224). In occupations, children express their inner impulses, interests, images, and ideas to the exterior world through interaction with social materials familiar to them from life in a social life environment. This kind of interaction enables them to make meaning concerning social materials and processes, which in turn enables guidance and direction of individual impulses. In short, occupation is a framework in which the social aspect controls self-expression. Therefore, occupations can serve as a mode of activity enabling self-expression through socially shared methods.

When occupations are thus viewed as self-expression activities, the expression takes place externally through the construction of materials. In Dewey's terms, occupations constitute "expressive and constructive activity" (*MW*1: 318); they are activities that express and activities that construct. Viewed psychologically, occupations are activities in which the self is expressed through the construction of materials. On this basis, we may consider "self-expression through the construction of materials" to be the methodological principle of occupation.

Structure of occupation

Next, let us clarify the structure of occupation as an educational method. To this end, this section considers occupation from the three aspects of process (time), psychology (interaction with materials), and society (human relations) to grasp the fundamental points and elements of each.

1. Process aspect

The process aspect views occupation through the passage of time. The fundamental point of the process aspect is the role of "'an experience' as inquiry."

An occupation is not a lineup of sporadic activities but a continuous, developmental process of exploring the questions arising from activities and accumulating meaning. This can be understood as what Dewey called "an experience." "An experience" creates the process and temporal frameworks of the occupation. "An experience" refers not to something that continues unchanged or veers off course, but to an experience with a dynamic wholeness from its start through its development to its conclusion (*LW*10: 42–43). Whether playing chess or attending a dinner, the situation will eventually reach a consummation, unless it is interrupted partway through. When experience along these lines includes the movement of the meaning of the previous experience becoming subsumed into the next action to create a whole, it may become "an experience." "An experience" is a process of activity whereby the meaning of objects is deepened, conserved, and accumulated through successive deeds, finally reaching the conclusion that renders the process complete (*LW*10: 45).

The process of occupation forms a whole that begins, develops, and ends. The beginning of the process is the impulse of self-expression, developed in inquiry using intelligence and concluded with the creation of a tangible product as the outcome—that is, "'an experience' as inquiry." Overall, this can be conceptualized as a process of "impulse–inquiry–product." Below, the elements of "'an experience' as inquiry" are discussed one by one.

(1) Impulse and interest

Dewey mentioned that every experience begins with an impulsion, rather as impulsion (*LW*10: 64). He considered the impulsiveness naturally present in children to be the root of the human life force, not a nuisance. Babies physically address the environments they are born into through impulsion, discovering what kind of world they are in and adjusting the self as they grow. The impulse of self-expression gives rise to occupation, becoming interest and driving the occupation to completion. Impulse is a fundamental component of occupation.

Dewey considered impulses or instincts that are social, constructive, investigative, or expressive to be educational and usable in schools, placing them at the starting point of occupations. He explained these impulses as follows.

First, there is the social instinct, the desire to recount one's own experience to others. As the impulse for conversation and communication, this includes the language instinct. Next is the constructive instinct, the desire for making. This appears in play, in movement, in gesture, and so on, and from there "seeks outlet in shaping materials into tangible forms and permanent embodiment" (*MW*1: 29). Third is the instinct of investigation. This develops from the combination of the constructive impulse with the conversational. When making something, children try various things. They like to do things and watch to see what will happen (*MW*1: 29). They want to tell people about what they have discovered. Fourth is the expressive impulse or, in other terms, the art instinct. This develops from the communication instinct and the constructive instinct. When making something with the constructive instinct, if given "a social motive, something to tell," an expression will result (*MW*1: 29–30). In occupations, children manifest these educational impulses and seek out continuous experiences based on their own desires.

The impulses that give rise to occupations do not disappear once they have served their purpose, but they are converted into interest through interaction with objects. Interest plays a larger part in occupations than simply a driving force.

Among its roles is the expression of the self. When impulse finds a specific object in the environment, it becomes interest. Finding an object means that the self has selected things in its environment, directed its attention to them as objects, and connected them to the environment. Individual sensibility plays a major part here. In this sense, interest can be grasped as the exercise of the "individual" on "society." Dewey considered "interest" and "self" two terms for the same concept (*MW9*: 361). When the self identifies with some object or idea, becoming entirely absorbed in the action in progress, interest is sure to be present (*MW7*: 159).

The second role is that of connecting objects within the environment, including human beings. Dewey explained the origin of the word "interest" as "what is *between*—that which connects two things otherwise distant" (*MW9*: 134); occupations founded on interest thus "articulate a vast variety of impulses, otherwise separate and spasmodic, into a consistent skeleton with a firm backbone" (*MW1*: 95). Interest connects and brings cohesion to the various elements composing interaction, driving experience from its start through its development to its conclusion with consistency.

(2) Logical problem-solving as inquiry

At this point, the interactions of occupations derived from impulse enter inquiry, where the intelligence functions. In occupations, when impulsive actions are ill adapted to the social environment, children realize that the situation is a problem and try various actions to adapt to the environment. They try to solve the problem. They discern the connection between the action and the consequence: "When I did this, this happened." Dewey mentioned that it is intelligence that works to connect the action (doing) and the consequence (undergoing). "Reflective thinking" is his term for the perception of the connection between the action and the consequence through intelligence (*MW9*: 151–152).

When this connection is perceived through reflective thinking, the connection takes on meaning. Dewey described the increase of meaning as "the increased perception of the connections and continuities of the activities in which we are engaged" (*MW9*: 82–83). As the connection between action and consequence takes on meaning through reflective thinking, the next action is given direction. This is the process of intellectualization of impulse through reflective thinking.

This process contains the essence of inquiry, the recovery from incompatibility to adaptation to the environment. The problem solving therein is governed by the perception of the logic in the relations among the objects experienced. Therefore, the process of transforming impulse into intelligence is also the process of logical problem-solving, accumulating the logical meaning of interactions with the environment through the reflective thinking of inquiry. Inquiry in occupation can thus be considered a process of logical problem-solving.

(3) Products as outcomes

The conclusion of "an experience" is not separate from the process leading to it but is the consummation of "a movement of anticipation and cumulation," with a rhythm like the ebb and flow of waves (LW10: 45).

The process of occupation also ends with the creation of an outcome. Because occupations are activities using tangible materials, their outcomes are "tangible and visible achievement" (MW9: 211). In this case, the meaning gained through the process is embodied in various actual objects, which may be called "products." Products are created by applying human labor to the natural resources of materials in the natural world. For instance, in occupations with sheep's wool and raw cotton, the threads made by manually separating the cotton fibers and the spinning tools may be called the products. These products are used as materials and tools for the next activity. When yarn is spun from wool, the yarn as the product creates the desire to weave on a loom, leading to the task of creating a loom to weave with. In short, the products of occupations are characteristically materials and tools that expand and deepen children's subsequent experiences.

2. Psychological aspect

The psychological aspect views occupation through the interaction between children and materials. Dewey describes the experience as follows. "Every experience is the result of interaction between a live creature and some aspect of the world in which he lives" (*LW*10: 50). In the experience of occupation, children interact with the materials that constitute the environment. Such interaction occurs in a way that interrelates mind and body, that is, in a psychosomatic way. The fundamental point of the psychological aspect is "logical thinking through the psychosomatic interaction between children and materials"

First, the interactions with the materials in occupations are characterized by the interrelation between the mind and body. Dewey viewed the body not as a physical substance but as a whole with the mind, an integrated "body-mind." When doing something, the active and affective element of acting with desire or purpose toward the object is essential (*MW*9: 285). Humans acquire knowledge through physically interacting with their environment based on their own desires and purposes. The knowledge thus acquired is a fusion with active and affective elements such as impulse, interest, and desire and not simply a matter of having learned about something. In short, knowledge based in the body is whole-person knowledge, comprising intelligence, sensibility, and will. Dewey identified the body as the foundation of perception, awareness, will, and emotion—that is, the foundation of human existence.

Experience in occupation was a physically active process of using the body to do something, not simply sitting and thinking. Dewey argued that analyzing and arranging facts could not be done inside one's head alone: "Men have to do something to the things when they wish to find out something; they have to alter conditions" (*MW*9: 284). This continuous grasp of the body and mind is what the psychosomatic way refers to.

There are three general functions of the body in occupation. First, the body serves as a passage for the release of internal interests. According to Dewey, when children "do things, and watch to see what will happen," setting their hands to something themselves, they are manifesting their interest (*MW*1: 29). Second, the body serves to express perceptions and emotions. Dewey argued that children learn and sense things through physical movement and express to the exterior world what they have learned and sensed likewise (*EW*5: 226). Third, the body visualizes the mind and enables social relations between children. Dewey revealed that expressive activities through physical exercise are given meaning through the re-actions of others (*EW*5: 226).

The second point here is that occupation is characterized by continuous interaction in a psychosomatic way on the axis of logic. Dewey cited "a balance between the intellectual and the practical phases of experience" as a fundamental point in the psychology of occupation (*MW*1: 92). Externally, occupations appear to be physical activities using the body's various organs; however, this use must be interrelated with intellectual thought such as observation, planning, and reflection. Children consider and perform their next actions by observing a situation, making a plan, carrying it out, and reflecting on the results. That is, children move forward with interaction based on the logic of the relation between doing and undergoing.

Based on the above considerations, the fundamental point of the psychological aspect of occupation is "logical thinking through the psychosomatic interaction between children and materials." Below are the elements of "logical thinking through the psychosomatic interaction between children and materials."

(1) Interaction of inner and outer materials

In the interaction in a psychosomatic way in occupation, the inner material is self-derived from impulse, and the outer material is the social material of the scope of social life. For instance, this may consist of the materials and processes of society and the surrounding natural environment as experienced in daily life. This may include wood, metal, the linen, cotton, and raw wool used in textile work; the tools used to card sheep's wool; the eggs used in cooking; the language used to convey experience; and the bridges and shops in town.

When these outer materials related to social life are made into teaching materials, what significance is attributed to them?

First, human fundamental common concerns center about food, shelter, and clothing, in addition to facilities for production and consumption such as stores and factories (*MW*9: 207). They embody not only the desire to stay alive (practical) but also the overall human desire to appreciate aesthetic qualities (aesthetic). Therefore, "they tap human instincts at a deep level (*MW*9: 207)."

Second, the content of occupations is linked with academic study and science. For example, gardening is not preparation to work as a gardener in the future. Gardening provides a means of approaching knowledge on the positions held by agriculture and horticulture in human history, in addition to their positions in the social mechanisms of today. It serves as a means of researching soil chemistry, the roles played by light, air, and moisture, and so on (*MW*9: 208), shifting children's interests to intellectual research into botany, such as plant germination and nutrient absorption (*MW*9: 208).

Third, occupations involve not only the content of academic study and science but also their methods. The experimental method emerged in the 17th century along with the progress of science. This method includes experiments such as dripping acid onto a stone to see what happens. Occupation is the most vital introduction to the scientific method of experiments (*MW*9: 210).

In short, because the materials handled in occupations are social materials, they are significant as teaching materials in the development of children's interests while involving content and methods leading to academic study and science.

(2) Perception of the logical connections between "doing" and "undergoing"

The interaction of inner and outer materials is guided by the logical connections between "doing" and "undergoing." In short, it constitutes logical thinking.

Upon interacting with outer materials, impulses become desires and are then converted into interests. Gaining a purpose through intelligence enables observation of objective conditions. Gaining meaning from the content observed, plans and execution follow. This process is driven by impulse and desire, and it is focused on the intellectual action of reflective thinking. Here the path of experience is traced, with the logical connections between means and consequences as its meaning. In occupation, "some perception of the relation of consequences to means" is characterized by the background support of feeling, the aspect of sensibility; however, this aspect remains in the background, with children expected to master this perception in the form of logical connections between means and consequences (*LW*13: 56–57).

Let us consider these interactions from the viewpoint of the connections between "doing" and "undergoing." For example, measuring the amount of grains to be used when cooking cereals (doing). When measuring various grains, children discover (undergo) that a cup of wheat and a cup of corn weigh different amounts, that is, volume and weight are not the same. They then discover that volume is a suitable measuring scale to find the amount of water needed for each grain (perception of logic). This concept is applied to the next activity, and finally, the children come up with a system of weights and measures on their own (Mayhew & Edwards: 278–279). The actions here are made continuous by the logic that connects things. Inquiry in observations progresses through the cycle of observing facts and acquiring ideas from them—a cycle thought to be led by logic. Thus, the connections of "doing" and "undergoing" in occupations are mainly perceived as logical connections.

(3) Multilayered thought structure of "body, image, and reflection"

The interactions in occupation are based in the body; they also call for intellectual logical thinking. Therefore, the thought structure of occupation has multiple layers, from the level of physical action to that of logical manipulation.

At the physical level, thought perceives the world through the "sensory-motor coordination" of hands and eyes. This is a form of thought observed in infants. They see an object and reach out to grab it, perceiving the object and the situation through their sense of the time required to grab it and the tactile sensation of the object itself. Dewey opined that these acts of conscious selection and arrangement already constitute the rudiments of thought (LW8: 281–282).

Next is thought that perceives the world through the "free representation" of signs and images. When a child plays horse with a broom, the visible object (the broom) is subordinated to the invisible one (the horse), enabling the child to expand their reality (LW8: 284–285). The stance here is one of interest in creating suggestions through signs and images and in embodying and freely assigning meaning to the real world. Dewey called this "playfulness" (LW8: 284). However, at these times, the child is not concerned with whether the broom is objectively a horse. The meaning here is subjective.

When they enter school, children can no longer be satisfied with subjective meaning: they become more interested in embodying and confirming the meaning in actual situations. In this sense, the essence lies in the connection between the means and the ends (*LW*8: 286–287), and significance is objectively confirmed in actual situations. In other words, a "reflection on means and ends" is carried out. Consecutive activities directed by ends also produce interest. Dewey called this the transition from play to work (*LW*8: 285).

Occupation is not simply a shift from one of the three forms of thought in human development noted above to another, but an accumulation of all three forms. Occupation can be considered to consist of "sensory-motor coordination," "free representation," and "reflection on means and ends," which compose the multilayered structure of the three forms of thought—"body, image, and reflection."

3. Social aspect

The social aspect of occupation is concerned with human relations. The fundamental point of the social aspect is "communication as the sharing of experience."

The social aspect can be grasped as rooted in the social instinct of communication, the desire to convey one's own experience to others. In Dewey's terms, communication means not a one-way transmission of information but "the way in which [people] come to possess things in common" (*MW*9: 7), that is, a means of exchanging and sharing experiences. For society to remain in existence, people are called on to exchange experiences and form communities through shared understanding of "aims, beliefs, aspirations, knowledge" (*MW*9: 7). Communication is a means of exchanging experiences, obtaining shared understanding, and forming communities.

Communication brings about changes in both the sender and the receiver. To state their experience clearly to others, the sender must take an objective view of their own experience. At the same time, "one has to assimilate, imaginatively, something of another's experience in order to tell him intelligently of one's own experience," calling for an attitude of empathy (*MW*9: 8-9). That is, the sender must adopt an intellectual and empathetic attitude toward their own experience. The receiver's experience is modified and expanded through gaining the new perspectives of others. In this sense, communication is considered educative (*MW*9: 9).

Based on the above, the fundamental point of the social aspect of occupation is "communication as the sharing of experience" in which the sender and the receiver share a give-and-take relationship (*MW*1: 35). Below are the elements of "communication as the sharing of experience."

(1) Communication in shared activities

Occupations are typical activities of social life, in which children share a goal and carry out a shared or conjoint activity (*MW*9: 35). However, according to Dewey, not all activities in which multiple children divide work among themselves with a common goal are shared activities. Shared activities involve the following conditions: (1) awareness of the common end, (2) interest in its completion, and (3) regulation of the activity with consideration for the shared end (*MW*9: 7–8). Dewey added that communication makes it possible to fulfill these conditions (*MW*9: 8). To explain this, he used the example of playing catch. If two people are simply throwing a ball back and forth mechanically, that is not a shared activity. However, when each becomes interested in the actions of the other and thereby interested in what they are doing themselves as connected with the action of the other (*MW*9: 34), the activity becomes a shared one, and the actions of both participants are socially directed (*MW*9: 36).

In other words, shared activities require both the emotion of interest and impulse toward achievement as well as the intellectual attitude of interacting with others with a end in mind. To this end, each person must know what the others are doing and inform the others of their own goal and what they are doing (*MW*9: 8). Therefore, shared activities call for physical as well as linguistic communication. This suggests that occupation requires a situation where children are face-to-face and look at each other.

According to Dewey, the capacity for social efficiency in a democratic society refers to the "capacity to share in a give and take of experience" (*MW*9: 127). This is precisely the ability to take part in shared activities through communication. which makes it easier to perceive others and convey one's own experience and enables one to sense others' interests. This is said to be the socialization of the mind (MW9: 127).

(2) Socialization of impulse and formation of an empathetic attitude

According to Dewey, participation in the shared activities of occupations controls children's inherent impulses and shapes their intellectual and moral dispositions. The control of impulse does not occur under physical compulsion. When performing a shared activity with a common end, the common understanding of what methods to use to accomplish the end serves to control individual actions (MW9: 32). The control of impulse arises through a common understanding among people in the same situation of the connection between means and ends and of their meaning.

Further, Dewey noted that internal control and socialization of impulse are a matter of emotion as well as of the intelligence to perceive the connection between means and ends in shared activities. According to Dewey, in shared activities, a child "not merely acts in a way agreeing with the actions of others, but, in so acting, the same ideas and emotions are aroused in him that animate the others" (MW9: 17). This means that he feels the success of his partner in the shared activity "as his success, its failure as his failure" (MW9: 18). This may be called an empathetic attitude. In occupations, participation in a shared activity socially intellectualizes impulse and cultivates an attitude of empathy toward others.

The concept of occupation as an educational method

This section summarizes the discussion above and educes from it the concept of occupation as an educational method.

First, the issue addressed by Dewey's educational philosophy is the "harmony of the individual with society." The principle for its realization in school education is the "connection between school and life." Occupation is an educational method intended to realize this principle. To realize the "connection between of school and life," occupation is positioned as a method of "education through life experience," which serves as the foundation for "education through symbols."

Life experience mainly consists of direct experience through the physical senses.

Given that direct experience enables the generation of meaning through real sensation, we may consider the essence of occupation as an educational method to be "direct experience as life experience." The realization of sense through direct experience brings reality back to school education. To bring this about, occupations employ the methodological principle of "self-expression through the construction of materials." This methodological principle realizes the self-expression impulse through constructing outer materials in the social life environment.

Next, the structure of occupation can be grasped from its "process, psychological, and social aspects" as follows.

The fundamental point of the process aspect is "'an experience' as inquiry." "An experience" involves the process from beginning through development to completion. In occupations this becomes the process of "impulse–inquiry–outcome." An inquiry beginning with impulse and interest develops as logical problem solving and concludes with the creation of a tangible product.

The fundamental point of the psychological aspect is "logical thinking through the psychosomatic interaction between children and materials." This is carried out through interactions of inner and outer (social) materials, in which the connection of "doing" and "undergoing" is grasped mainly as a logical connection. To move forward with these interactions, the mode of activity of occupation adopts a multilayered thought structure of "body, image, and reflection."

The fundamental point of the social aspect is "communication as the sharing of experience." In occupation as a shared activity with a common end, individual experiences are exchanged and meaning is shared. The shared activity socializes impulse and cultivates an empathetic attitude.

This structure of occupation as an educational method thus involves a framework in which the fundamental points are "'an experience' as inquiry" for the process aspect, "logical thinking through the psychosomatic interactions between children and materials" for the psychological aspect, and "communication as the sharing of experience" for the social aspect.

Based on the above, the concept of occupation as an educational method can be educed as follows. Occupation is a shared activity involving shared experience. In

this activity, impulse is stimulated, and children use their bodies to construct social materials. Because the construction of materials in the exterior world is
interrelated with the inner mind, the construction of materials serves to express
the interior, such as individual thoughts, images, and feelings. Because the construction of materials in the exterior world is interrelated with the expression of
the inner self, this self is also reconstructed along with the construction of materials. Given that the reconstruction of the inner self is deliberate rather than
accidental, occupation can be considered an educational method that brings about
this reconstruction. In summary, the concept of occupation as an educational
method arrived at is "an educational method that reconstructs the inner self by
constructing outer materials, through the psychosomatic interaction between children and materials deriving from impulse, in shared activities."

Notes

1. "Constructive occupation" is used in the title of Chapter 14, Section 3 of *How We Think* (*LW*8:
290), and "active occupation" in the title of Chapter 15, Section 2 of *Democracy and Education*
(*MW*9: 202). "Constructive work" and "manual training" are used as synonyms or descriptions of
occupation in Dewey's papers related to the Laboratory School (*EW*5: 231, *MW*1: 231).
2. The examples have been summarized by the author from Mayhew & Edwards: 82–83 and *MW*1:
30–31.

Chapter

2

The Connection Between Artistic Experience and Occupation

Chapter 1 clarified the concept of occupation as an educational method. Chapter 2 theoretically clarifies what kind of experience "artistic experience" is and, based thereon, discusses how artistic experience connects to occupation.

Essence, methodological principles, and structure of artistic experience

Experience in artistic construction activity is "artistic experience." With Dewey's *Art as Experience* as the main reference text, this part theoretically clarifies what kind of experience "artistic experience" is. To this end, this part begins by showing where the essence of artistic experience is to be found and what methodological principles make experience artistic. It then clarifies the structure of artistic experience through the process, psychological, and social aspects.

Essence and methodological principles of artistic experience

1. What is artistic experience?

(1) Experience

In general, experience is categorized with terms such as scientific, contemplative/philosophical, religious, aesthetic, and moral. However, Dewey did not discuss experience using these categories or divisions. For him, "experience" is the mutual interaction of organisms with the environment for the purpose of staying alive. In short, it is life itself. From there, certain aspects become dominant in response to the interests and ends of the organism, characterizing the overall experience. Adjectives such as scientific, contemplative/philosophical, religious, aesthetic, moral, and so on are simply attached to the experience in retrospect (*LW*10: 44). Regardless of what adjective is used, experience comprises a whole, unifying all aspects of mutual interaction between the organism and the environment.

(2) "An experience" and "aesthetic experience"

According to Dewey, aesthetics exist within experience (*LW*10: 16). "Experience" is the interaction between organisms and the environment. There, the mutual interaction of the organism "doing" something to the environment and "undergoing" something from the environment continues in a rhythm like that of breathing in and out (*LW*10: 62). With the rhythm of breathing, experience is truly life itself.

When resistance or conflict of some kind occurs, the organism stops to resolve the problem, reflects on the situation, and thus acquires conscious intent. However, this process is often prevented from reaching consummation by interference or distraction. Conversely, when mutual interaction follows the smooth course, reaches consummation and becomes complete, it amounts to what Dewey referred to as "*an* experience" (*LW*10: 42).

"An experience" begins with an interior impulse or desire in the organism and reaches its final consummation through internal integration, taking on a dynamic unity. This situation has an individual "quality" that pervades the entire experience (*LW*10: 43). This pervasive quality makes the experience a whole, giving it individuality different from that of other experiences (*LW*10: 42).

When "experience" acquires the unity of "*an* experience" through internal integration, it acquires an aesthetic quality. Dewey stated that "an experience" with internal integration and fulfillment is in itself "aesthetic," finding aesthetic quality in the movement that evokes unity in experience, rendering it "an experience" (*LW*10: 45). Importantly, this movement is not simply forward action but a movement with the alternating rhythm of "doing" and "undergoing," which accumulates meaning as it moves toward consummation (*LW*10: 45). Dewey considered "aesthetic quality" in this internal movement, rhythmically unifying experience as it sets a direction toward consummation. He argued that scientific experience may also have aesthetic quality, if the conditions leading to its conclusion are aggregated and made complete to form "an experience" (*LW*10: 80).

Here we see Dewey's unique attitude toward "beauty." When Dewey mentioned "beauty," he did not discuss "the beauty" as a substance. Rather, he identified aesthetic quality in the movement creating an ordered and complete whole through unifying the elements of various experiences. He stated that it is "the aesthetic" that draws attention to, enhances, and develops this aesthetic quality (*LW*10: 52-23).

(3) "Aesthetic experience" and "artistic experience"

In this way, rather than defining beauty as a sublime value to be pursued, Dewey considered aesthetic quality in "an experience," which may arise even from simple, everyday experiences when they acquire order and completion through internal integration.

Is "an experience" always an "aesthetic experience," then? Certainly not. It depends on the interest and purpose of the experience. Even if possessed of aesthetic quality, if its interest and purpose lie in the practical or intellectual rather than aesthetic aspects, "an experience" is mainly a practical or intellectual experience and cannot be said to be "*distinctively* [a]esthetic" (*LW*10: 61–62). What experiences, then, can be clearly identified "aesthetic experiences"? Aesthetic experiences in Dewey's terms are those in which the aesthetic quality, more than any other characteristic, dominates the whole. That is, to be clearly considered an "aesthetic experience," it must be "an experience" with aesthetic quality to its interest and purpose, which dominate the experience as a whole. Dewey positioned the experience of art as the perfect archetype of "aesthetic experience" (*LW*10: 61–62), recognizing therein originality and value not found in any other experiences and positioning this form of experience as the most valuable (*LW*1: 8). This book refers to experience whose interest and purpose are found in the aesthetic quality itself as "artistic experience."[1]

2. Essence and methodological principles of artistic experience

(1) Interest and purpose of artistic experience

How does an experience of art as an aesthetic-experience, that is to say an artistic experience, differ from a scientific, religious, or contemplative experience? First, the interest and purpose of the experience are different. In artistic experience, the interest and purpose are not practical or logical, but aesthetic, that is, focused on the aesthetic quality itself.

According to Dewey, scientists' interests and purposes are "intellectual," while artists' are "[a]esthetic" (*LW*10: 61). Dewey identified the differences thus created to appear in the different emphases and tempos of the rhythm of "loss of integration with environment and recovery of union" amid the interactions of organisms with their environment (*LW*10: 21).

Scientists are interested in the situations of lost integration with the environment, that is, the problems, where they work to resolve resistance and tension. Their emphasis is on the aspect of problem-solving. When the problem has been resolved, they adopt it as a tool for work on the next problem. Therefore, their tempo is faster.

Artists, on the other hand, are interested in the situations where integration has been lost and union is recovered. Rather than make haste to resolve the resistance or tension of these situations, they cultivate these aspects (*LW*10: 21). Therefore, their tempo is slower.

What does it mean to cultivate resistance or tension? While Dewey did not provide an explanation for this, the author believed that it referred not to hastening toward a solution but to find interest and enjoyment in the process of trial and error in searching for a solution, exploring various possibilities. Dewey explained that artists enjoy cultivating the recovery of union with the environment not because of the resistance and tension in themselves but because of the possibilities they provide for vivid perception of a unified, overall experience (*LW*10: 21). This may be interpreted as follows. To realize union with the environment, artists sense the quality of the present situation and transform it into a quality of overall harmony. The solution they adopt, while only a partial attempt, affects and changes the quality of the entire situation. The overall quality of the new, changed situation provides hints toward the possibility of new solutions and concepts. In short, because resistance and tension are expected to stimulate creativity, artists attempt to cultivate them.

(2) The materials of artistic experience

Because their interests and purposes are different, scientists and artists handle different subject-matter and thus different materials. Dewey documented the following regarding the difference in materials.

Artists adopt the qualities of things of direct experience as their subject-matter (*LW*10: 80). The materials of their experience are perceptual materials having these qualities. Interested in the qualitative meanings produced by qualitative relations (meanings and values that can be expressed only through direct visual or auditory properties), artists work to express these meanings through qualitative media (colors, sounds, etc.). Therefore, they express the qualities of things of direct experience with qualitative media, addressing relationships of quality. They express and individualize meaning, thus constructing experience (*LW*10: 89–90).

Scientists remain a step back from the qualities of things of direct experience, handling them through the medium of symbols (numbers, signs, etc.). Here the materials of inquiry become conceptual. Scientists are interested in the meanings abstracted by symbols, such as using the notation H_2O to show the conditions under which water is generated. Therefore, they state the qualities of things of direct experience with symbols, addressing relationships of symbols. They describe meaning as the conditions created by perception of a thing or situation in a certain context, generalizing it and using it as a signpost to experience (*LW*10: 89–90).

This difference in materials constitutes the essential difference between scientific experience and artistic experience. Scientists handle the aspect of observing direct experience with symbols, while artists attempt to approach its qualities directly. Therefore, the products of experience are "knowledge" as a conceptual system for scientists and "artworks" for artists.

(3) Essence and methodological principles of artistic experience

As we have seen here, there are two fundamental elements distinguishing artistic experience from other experience: the interest and purpose of artistic experience lying in the aesthetic quality of experience and the consequent use of qualitative materials.

What does this actually mean? In artistic experience, the materials of experience are qualitative. The qualities of things experienced directly through the physical senses are expressed with perceptual materials having qualities such as color and sound. That is, the qualities experienced are grasped directly and instinctively, without the mediation of symbols or signs, and they are expressed with qualitative media.

The purpose of this is complete unity of the self with the environment. Expressing the qualities experienced with qualitative media implies the direct interaction of organisms with their environment, without the mediation of symbols. Direct interaction of the self and the environment without intermediation enables unity of the self and the environment. According to Dewey, because artists, unlike scientists, think in qualitative media without the mediation of symbols, "the terms lie so close to the object [they are] producing that they merge directly into it" (*LW*10: 21). In short, because artists use qualitative media, they can embody their self directly in things. Because there is no indirect mediation, the situation of complete unity between the environment and the self is easier to bring about. This is the "recovery of the union with the environment" unique to artistic experience, differentiating it from scientific experience; it is thus that artists find the unique satisfaction of consummation in aesthetic experience. In artistic experience, the union and integration of the self and the environment is itself the purpose.

Based on the above, artistic experience is aesthetic experience whose purpose is the creation of qualitative relationships with aesthetic qualities, using qualitative materials. This is the process from the beginning to the development of the conclusion of experience, which accumulates the meaning creating qualitative relationships and constructing and completing tangible artworks. The essence of this kind of artistic experience lies in "aesthetic experience as qualitative experience," which aims for the unity of the self and the environment. The methodological principle creating artistic experience from experience lies in the "expression of qualities of experience through the construction Of qualitative materials."

The process aspect of artistic experience

1. Expression as "an experience"

Artistic experience is "an experience," carried out as an act of "expression."[2] This section, with *Art as Experience* as its main reference text, clarifies the process aspect of artistic experience from the perspective of expression. How is expression developed as "an experience"?

Dewey grasped the act of expression as the interaction between "inner" and "outer" materials. Inner materials include images, observation, memory, emotion, and so on. Outer materials, which are shaped into artworks, include marble, paint, words, and so on, as materials evoking qualities (*LW*10: 81). In Dewey's words, "As a painter places pigment upon the canvas, or imagines it placed there, his ideas and feeling are also ordered" (*LW*10: 81). The inner and outer materials work upon each other to undergo mutual change. Therefore, according to Dewey, expression is not the outward show of preexisting inner materials to be expressed. By changing the form of the outer materials, the internal world composed of the inner materials is also changed and given shape. In other words, the principle of expression is the changing form and reconstruction of the inner and outer worlds through the interaction between inner and outer materials. Next, let us consider the conditions for expression to constitute "an experience."

2. Impulsion and resistance

(1) Impulsion

"Every experience, of slight or tremendous import, begins with an impulsion, rather *as* an impulsion." (*LW*10: 64). For Dewey, impulsion is the origin of

experience. Therefore, it is the origin of expression as well. Impulsion is a movement outward and forward of the whole organism into its environment, "the craving
of the living creature for food" (*LW*10: 64). When an organism senses something in-
congruous in its environment and feels a need, impulsion propels it forward into
the environment.

(2) Resistance

However, the forward progress of impulsion alone is simply the release of action,
not expression. Dewey argued that impulsion must encounter resistance to enter
the channel to expression. Resistance refers to the things blocking an organism's
way when it enters a new environment. When impulsion encounters resistance of
some kind, it is forced to go backward (re-flection) rather than forward, creating internal tension. Here "the live creature becomes aware of the intent implicit in its
impulsion... Blind surge has been changed into a purpose; instinctive tendencies
are transformed into contrived undertakings. The attitudes of the self are informed
with meaning." (*LW*10: 65). That is, the encounter of impulsion with resistance in
the outer materials of the environment creates reflection, upon which the organism
discovers the purpose and meaning of what the self latent within the impulsion
wants to do, in other words, being aware of the self.

In this way, the necessary prerequisite for impulsion to enter the channel to expression is the encounter with resistance upon moving forward into the
environment.

3. Establishment of expression

When impulsion encounters resistance, resulting in reflection, a "double change"
is generated. The double change refers to the change of impulsion via expressive
media into a substance with form, along with the simultaneous change in which
the junction of new and old experience acts as a recreation. Dewey documented that
this double change is the essence of expression (*LW*10: 66). Below is a discussion of
the double change.

(1) Expressive media

To cause impulsion to enter the channel to expression rather than simply releasing energy, outer materials—that is, expressive media—enabling it to take on a substantial form are needed. When impulsion encounters resistance, resulting in reflection, the organism becomes aware of its own needs, purpose, and intent and attempts to realize them through the use of outer materials as resistance in the environment. The outer materials selected as a method at this point become the expressive media. Impulsion takes shape and is embodied in the outer world through attaining expressive media (*LW*10: 65–66).

In this way, expressive media is not bestowed by another from outside but was there to begin with. The "materials" constituting the situation of resistance transform into the "expressive media". That is, when the materials constituting resistance are used as a method for pursuing the organism's own purpose, they become expressive media.

(2) The junction of old and new experience

As noted above, impulsion acquires expressive media when encountering resistance, resulting in reflection. However, this alone does not lead to the establishment of expression. At the same time, the junction of old and new experience must take place through reflection.

Dewey stated that when impulsion encounters and attempts to overcome resistance, meanings from past experience are evoked and assimilated with the current experience to be revived as new meanings. According to Dewey, when impulsion is turned back by resistance, it leads to even deeper insight into its end and method (*LW*10: 66). At this time, the meanings of past experiences are recalled and assimilated into the new experience. Further, "[this] junction of the new and old is not a mere composition of forces, but is a re-creation in which the present impulsion gets form and solidity while the old, the "stored", material is literally revived, given new life and soul through having to meet a new situation" (*LW*10: 66). The junction of old and new experiences represents the meanings of past experience flowing into the current experience, creating new meanings there.

Let us review the above. Upon the encounter of impulsion with resistance, the doer stops to reflect on their own experience. Here, a double change is generated: an outer change in which impulsion acquires media and takes on external shape, embodied in a form and substance, and an inner change of recreation via the junction of past and present experience. Dewey argued that this double change transforms an activity into an act of expression, wherein he understood the essence of expression (*LW*10: 66). Resistance generates this double change and establishes expression. Therefore, the encounter of impulsion with resistance is essential for expression.

(3) Modes of response of the doer

Given that expression is concomitant with the conditions of impulsion, resistance, expressive media, and the junction of old and new experience, there is one more required condition: the modes of response of the doer.

Dewey cited two of these modes of responses (*LW*10: 103). The first is motor dispositions previously formed. "To know what to look for and how to see it is an affair of readiness on the part of motor equipment ... It is necessary that there be ready defined channels of motor response" (*LW*10: 103–104). The example given is the physical response of a hunter when a deer suddenly appears. Dewey mentioned that this situation requires a physical response of the whole organism: brain, senses, and muscular system.

Second, in collaboration with the first, is the response of meanings and values extracted from prior experiences in response to the materials of expression currently present: "meanings and values extracted from prior experiences and funded in such a way that they fuse with the qualities directly presented in the work of art" (*LW*10: 104). Without this response in the doer, the present materials for expression will remain objective materials. Writing that "[i]magination is the only gateway through which these meanings can find their way into a present interaction" (*LW*10: 276), Dewey observed that imagination functions to close the distance between past and present experiences. If the doer does not put their imagination to use in a response extracting the meaning and values from past experiences, expression will not be established. Dewey stated that through these two modes of response on the part of the doer, impulsion can be led into the indirect channel of expression rather than being directly dissipated.

4. Artworks as products

When "an experience" is consummated as expression, the product it creates is an artwork.

According to Dewey, in intellectual experiences such as science and contemplation, the product is a "conclusion," "as a formula or as a 'truth'." Extracted from experience, these can be applied individually "as factor and guide in other inquiries" (*LW*10: 61). Thought in intellectual experience is mainly logical. The materials of this logical thinking are signs and symbols, without individual qualities. Therefore, the conclusions drawn from combinations of signs and symbols can be used anywhere freely, distinct from the situation which formed them.

However, "[i]n a work of art there is no such single self-sufficient deposit. The end, the terminus, is significant not by itself but as the integration of the parts" (*LW*10: 61). The terminus comes as part of a process possessed of a beginning, a development, and an end. Further, this process accumulates meaning as the qualities of the previous interactions permeate the following interactions. Events do not simply happen one after the next. They accumulate meaning, leading into the following event. Dewey stated that artists "must at each point retain and sum up what has gone before as a whole and with reference to a whole to come" (*LW*10: 63), arguing that only art can express the essence and significance of this cumulative process (*LW*10: 49).

That is, the products of artistic experience are not independently significant as tools to be used on the next occasion but significant as the individual consummation of the cumulative process from beginning to end of the experience. The process and products of artistic experience are identical, which is a characteristic of experience of this kind.

The psychological aspect of artistic experience

1. Qualitative thinking through the psychosomatic interaction

Next, let us discuss the psychological aspect of artistic experience. The fundamental point of the psychological aspect of artistic experience is "qualitative thinking through the psychosomatic interaction."

Artistic experience involves using the hands to change the form of materials immediately to consider the next action in response to the results of the first. This is a psychosomatic interaction. This interaction can also be viewed with the use of the hands as production and the response to the result as perception. Dewey noted that while the active or "doing" phase of art (manipulating clay, applying paint, and so on) is more prominent, it is in fact the passive "undergoing" phase that leads to production:

> Man whittles, carves, sings, dances, gestures, molds, draws, and paints. The doing or making is artistic when the perceived result is of such a nature that *its* qualities *as perceived* have controlled the question of production. (*LW*10: 55)

The passive phase is concerned with the observation, perception, and enjoyment indicated by the word "aesthetic." For example, an artist painting on a canvas is active or "doing," while their perception of the result is passive or "undergoing." If the result of the brushstroke is not what they had in mind, the artist considers their next step. The image in their mind may also be recreated anew at this point, leading to new attempts at expression. In either case, the "doing" of the artist's next step is considered in its relations to "undergoing" and to the artwork as a whole.

In this way, with regard to the connection of "doing" and "undergoing" in the artistic experience, it is the passive phase concerned with "undergoing" or perception that creates the integrity of the experience. Without "undergoing," "doing" would become diffusive. Therefore, Dewey argued that "[t]he artist embodies in himself the attitude of the perceiver while he works" (*LW*10: 55). This suggests that in artistic experience, the connection between "doing" and "undergoing" is extremely intimate. The two are directly linked by perception, without mediation. This "intimate union of doing and undergoing" can be viewed as a characteristic of artistic experience (*LW*10: 58).

This connection between "doing" and "undergoing" unique to artistic experience is created by "qualitative thinking." As the artist applies their brush to the canvas, they respond to the result with attention to the aesthetic quality of whether overall harmony is achieved and proceed to the next stroke, connecting "doing" and "undergoing." With regard to this connection, the artist has "an immediate sense of things in perception as belonging together or as jarring; as reenforcing or as interfering" (*LW*10: 56). In this way, they create their artwork while qualitatively examining the connection between "doing" and "undergoing." This is "qualitative thinking." Artists carry out qualitative thinking, mutually connecting the various qualities created by the interaction of active and passive, to shape their works. While on the other hand, in scientific and contemplative experience, the laws and concepts represented by signs and symbols are connected, while sensing elsewhere the qualities created by the connection of facts. This is "logical thinking," which creates connections via logic.

Based on the above, we see that the important point of the psychological aspect of artistic experience is "qualitative thinking through psychosomatic interaction." Below are the elements of "qualitative thinking through psychosomatic interaction."

2. Interaction of inner and outer (qualitative) materials

(1) The double change of inner and outer materials

As noted in the previous section, psychosomatic interaction is practiced through the interaction in expressive activities of inner materials such as emotions and ideas with outer materials such as marble, hues, or sound. Important here is the fact that inner and outer materials are linked as change is worked upon them (*LW*10: 81). According to Dewey, to shape artworks, marble must be chipped or paint applied, changing shape. At this point, "the side of 'inner' materials, images, observations, memories and emotions" must also be re-formed (*LW*10: 81).

Neither is transformed in an instant: rather, the change of form requires time. According to Dewey, in expressive activities, the outer physical materials are natural or perhaps native, primitive, or habitual (*LW*10: 69). These "materials" are changed and reformed to become "expressive media." To change and reform expressive media, continuous interaction is required. When the inner and outer materials are organized in organic mutual connection (*LW*10: 81), something new outside, that is an artwork, is created. This is the result of the operation in which both attain a form and order that did not previously exist (*LW*10: 71).

(2) Emotion

Although art is generally considered the expression of emotion, Dewey considered a different view. "It is selective of material and directive of its order and arrangement. But it is not *what* is expressed" (*LW*10: 75). Dewey considered the role of emotion to be found in the selection and organization of materials where inner and outer materials interact. The selection of materials by emotion means that when emotion finds an experienced emotional affinity in materials that appear random from the outside, it evokes and unifies this affinity to bestow thereon a qualitative unity (*LW*10: 49, 75). "[Emotional energy] evokes, assembles, accepts, and rejects memories, images, observations, and works them into a whole toned throughout by the same immediate emotional feeling" (*LW*10: 160). Emotion collates the selected materials, directs their order and arrangement, and shapes them.

In this way, when emotion is not directly dissipated but spent indirectly to find and bestow order on materials—that is, when following an indirect channel to expression—an emotion that begins coarsely or vaguely is transformed by objective materials, resulting in objectivizing and consummating the emotion itself as an aesthetic emotion (*LW*10: 83–85).

3. Perception of the qualitative connections between "doing" and "undergoing"

As noted above, the thinking that connects the interactions of inner and outer materials in artistic experience is "qualitative thinking." Dewey described the thinking of artists as follows. Although not generally considered to do so, artists think as intently and penetratingly as scientists (*LW*10: 52). However, while the materials of scientists' experiences are signs and symbols without qualities of their own, those of artists' experiences are qualities in themselves, so artistic thinking differs from its scientific counterpart. Artists' thinking involves perceiving the connection between doing and, as its result, undergoing as qualitative. To perceive the qualitative connection between "doing" and "undergoing," tremendous observation and intelligence come into play (*LW*10: 56–57). By perceiving this connection, artists are able to anticipate the next action and discover what direction their work is going (*LW*10: 56–57). This is the qualitative thinking that creates qualitative connections among qualitative materials such as sound and color.

As a satisfactory artwork is created by direct perception through this kind of qualitative thinking, "doing" and "undergoing" complement one another reciprocally, cumulatively, and continuously (*LW*10: 56–57). Here the perception of the qualitative connection between "doing" and "undergoing" leads to the generation of qualitative meaning.

4. Expression of qualitative meaning

As noted above, Dewey did not consider art as an expression of emotion. What is it, then, that art expresses? According to Dewey, it expresses "an intimate union of the features of present existence with the values that past experience have incorporated in personality" (*LW*10: 78). That is, the meanings and values of past experience flow into and meld with present experience, creating new meanings and values (*LW*10: 66). Art expresses these newly created meanings and values. The same applies to appreciation as well as to production. In observation as well, through attaining "meanings and values extracted from prior experiences and funded in such a way that they fuse with the qualities directly presented in the work of art" (*LW*10: 104), appreciation acts as the "expression" of the perceiver.

If the meanings and values contained in past experiences are not joined with present actions, the actions of applying red paint to a canvas or creating sound by beating a drum would be simply acts of whimsy, evaporating into meaninglessness. These acts become acts of expression through the melding of past and present experiences. Dewey indicated a gap between the past and the present. It is imagination that leaps this gap to connect the past and present (*LW*10: 276).

Meaning in the sense discussed here is the qualitative meaning that cannot be expressed in words or symbols (*LW*10: 80). The author understands this as follows. We experience various qualities in our daily lives. When a vivid sunset shows itself in the window at the end of the day, we do not observe the fine graduations of hue in the clouds and sky simply as a spectacle: rather, we enjoy them based on the meanings and values in the contexts of our own lives. However, this kind of qualitative experience is easily lost and forgotten amid our everyday work. It is artistic experience that evokes and shapes the meanings of these past qualitative experiences. Dewey expressed this as follows. "What it does is to concentrate and enlarge an immediate experience. The formed matter of [a]esthetic experience directly *expresses*, in other words, the meanings that are imaginatively evoked" (*LW*10: 277). That is, "science states meanings; art expresses them" (*LW*10: 90).

This is a reference to the raison d'être of art. "The work of art has a unique *quality*, but that it is that of clarifying and concentrating meanings contained in scattered and weakened ways in the material of other experiences" (*LW*10: 90). We may interpret this to mean that art shapes and concentrates qualities that appear scattered and weak in everyday experience, expressing their qualitative meanings.

Artistic experience involves interactions that evoke the qualitative meanings accumulated in this way within everyday experience and express them in materials through qualitative thinking.

The social aspect of artistic experience

1. Communication of quality as the sharing of experience

Dewey held that art was a medium of communication rather than something confined within the individual, considering it a public matter open to society. Communication in Dewey's terms was not simply a one-way transmission but the "sharing of experience."

Dewey mentioned that to enable the sharing of experience, the sender must simultaneously hold the point of view of the recipient. Nothing will be shared with the recipient if the sender simply expresses their desires, emotions, or notions as they feel. The sender must take an objective view of their own experience, "seeing it as another would see it" and putting it into "such form that [the recipient] can appreciate its meaning" (*MW*9: 8-9).

In the case of art, the sender is the producer and the recipient is the perceiver; their relationship accords with that of communication as the sharing of experience. In the production of art, the producer must take the perceiver's point of view in expression. Likewise, in appreciation of the artwork, the perceiver is called on to recreate their own experience through interaction with the work, rather than simply looking at it (*LW*10: 60). In this way, given that the producer and the perceiver share their mutual experience with the artwork as commonality/medium, Dewey held that art is a form of communication. Naturally, "sharing" in this sense does not mean that the perceiver receives the producer's experience wholesale. The experiences of the producer and the perceiver are shared *based on their respective interests and perspectives*, through continuous interaction with the artwork.

Taking this stance, artistic experience appears to be an interaction between producer and perceiver with the shared object of the artwork as the medium, meaning that it can be understood to be communication as the sharing of experience. The meaning of the work, then, is not linguistic but qualitative, meaning that the communication is qualitative as well.

Based on the above, the important point of the social aspect of artistic experience is "communication of quality as the sharing of experience." Below are the elements of "the communication of quality as the sharing of experience."

2. Communication of quality between producer and perceiver with public artworks as the medium

Why can multiple people share experiences with art as their medium? Dewey explained that "The *material* out of which a work of art is composed belongs to the common world rather than to the self" (*LW*10: 112). The producer transforms familiar public materials into a new substance through their intelligence and sen-sibility, and the perceiver likewise perceives the work by reconstructing familiar materials into new things in the same way (*LW*10: 112). That is, art may be under-stood as the activity of transforming public materials through the exertion of the self, representing them to the public world.

Further, this kind of communication through art is considered more universal than communication through language, thus endowing art with a unique signifi-cance. This significance is the way art essentially enables the junction of nature and humanity and of humanity with one another (*LW*10: 275).

Art has the power to bring about "the union of man with one another" in our common humanity (*LW*10: 275). Thanks to this power, we are capable of communi-cation with faraway people of differing cultures and ethnicities. Dewey suggested that as a hint toward understanding the art of other ethnicities, "art is expressive of a deep-seated attitude of adjustment" between humanity and its environment (*LW*10: 335). Understanding the art of other ethnicities is tantamount to communi-cation with alien people whose languages, cultures, and modes of behavior are different. Art is an expression of humanity's stance toward the question of how best to adapt to the environment, an issue that lies at the root of experience. Here, rather than focusing on surface-level differences, we are called on to imagine oth-ers' experience and walk in their shoes to grasp this stance at the root of experience. The communication of art enables us to join our own experiences with those of others at the deep dimension of this stance at the root of experience, expanding our own experiences. In short, we can link our own and others' experiences in a continuum.

Based on the above, Dewey suggested the possibility in art for sharing beyond the barriers between people of different cultures. Although difficult with communi-cation through language, this can be accomplished with communication through art (*LW*10: 338).

3. Formation of publicness through sharing qualities of the public world

The stance noted above of the understanding of art of different ethnicities relates to the efforts toward agreement through communication between people of different values and opinions. That is to say, while the understanding of art involves individual works, the deeper the dimension of this understanding, the farther it goes beyond individuality toward a common understanding between people, which is possessed of a social nature. Dewey argued that "works of art are the only media of complete and unhindered communication between man and man" (LW10: 110). Art takes the form of the highest communication, superseding language, because it is composed of "the common qualities of the public world" (LW10: 275). Artistic experience makes it possible to sense in concentrated form the qualities located in the depths of everyday existence. Dewey expressed this as follows.

> The function of art has always been to break through the crust of conventionalized and routine consciousness. Common things, a flower, a gleam of moonlight, the song of a bird, not things rare and remote, are means with which the deeper levels of life are touched so that they spring up as desire and thought. This process is art. (LW2: 349–350)

Because art functions to express the interiority of life experience, Dewey observed the formation of publicness in the communication of art. Dewey's point may be that through artistic experience, by sensing the qualities of shared humanity that permeate the deep levels of the lives led by people appearing to be different on the surface, an empathetic attitude creating a continuum between the self and others is formed, as is the perception of coexistence of the self and others—that is, publicness. Because art is an experience sensing and expressing the qualities of the world we live in, we are able to communicate beyond language with art as the medium. This derives from the experience of art as qualitative communication.

Continuity from occupations to artistic experience

Above, we have discussed what artistic experience is. Dewey's views on art held that the source of artistic experience is in life experience and that the two are thus continuous. Where, then, is the continuity from life experience to artistic experience? Let us look at this issue from the perspective of school education.

Arts education at the Laboratory School

1. Problems of arts education at the Laboratory School

Dewey stated that in principle, "drawing and music ... represent the culmination, the idealization, the highest point of refinement of all the work carried on" (MW1: 52), placing the arts at the pinnacle of the curriculum. This was due to his belief in art as an experience that melded the body and the mind, endowing things with spiritual meaning and expression (MW1: 53).

However, in a letter of 1900, Dewey wrote that the Laboratory School had failed to realize the ideal of arts education (Mayhew & Edwards: 361), judging that arts education there had not succeeded. He did not mention the reason for this failure. Why was the Laboratory School unable to realize arts education that Dewey would have found satisfactory?

The author felt that the reason lay in the Laboratory School's failure to grasp art as "experience."

Occupations as life experience lay at the core of study at the Laboratory School, but its arts education was positioned more as a subject in which experts provided instruction in expressive skills than as a field of study continuous with occupations.[3] In particular, music was considered almost entirely unrelated to occupations. The director of music was Calvin Brainerd Cady, a teacher at the Chicago Conservatory, and the practical teaching was done by his student May Root Kern. "Expression" in Cady's terms involved having children hum the melodies that came to mind for them. Kern described this as playing short melodies repeatedly to children from as early on as possible, familiarizing them with "a melodic conception through repetitions. Having understood, [they possess] a mental picture which [they seek] to express by humming or singing." This is the "expression of the aesthetic impulse." So as not to lose their grasp on the melodic conception, they would want to learn the symbols of sheet music (Kern: 33). The grounding for these musical expressions consisted of conceptual study of the elements of music (melody, rhythm, and harmony). Here, expression is not connected to life but comes to consummation only within the world of music.

The reports on practice in music focus on instruction in skills. For instance, "There being in this chorus a considerable proportion of children unable to sing a connected melody correctly, perfection in detail is impossible ... The special aims, other than familiarity with good songs and the memorizing of texts, have been bodily poise, deep breathing, careful enunciation, and a pure quality of tone" (Kern: 34). The class outcome was to be the formation of a chorus of selected singers, who would be trained as a model choir to promote the Laboratory School's music education (Kern: 34).

In classes with this kind of emphasis on performance, naturally the variation in musical ability between children was notable. Kern describes struggling to cope with this variation as a teacher. Tone-deaf children were given individual lessons in pitch (Kern: 34–35). No relation can be seen in the music class records between individual children's life experience and expression: the classes had wandered far afield of Dewey's philosophy of expressing the children's experiences.

The problems with arts education at the Laboratory School as noted above are thought to have lain in its approach as "skills education for expression", rather than "education expressing experience".

2. Overcoming the problems

The problems at the Laboratory School discussed above suggest that they might be overcome by approaching expression as "experience" rather than as an issue of technique or skill. To do so, expression must be understood as the interaction of doing and undergoing. At the Laboratory School, expression was understood as outward doing, provoking an awareness of the need to refine visible actions and thus developing a bias toward skill instruction from the outside. It is important to consider expression not as the aspect of doing alone but as the interaction of doing and undergoing, that is, as "experience."

This reveals the continuity from life experience to artistic experience. Dewey considered art as continuous with life experience: a continuity not of the subject but of experience itself. He found this continuity in the qualities permeating experience. Our experience is composed not of random things but permeated throughout with certain qualities, which meld with the elements and things of experience (*LW*12: 73-74). Art is the extraction, concentration, and expression of these qualities of experience (*LW*10: 198-199).

However, at the Laboratory School at the time, we may guess that the existence of the qualitative aspect of the experience of occupations was not consciously or perceptually handled. To relate occupations to artistic experience, we must consider this qualitative aspect.

Continuity from occupations to artistic experience

The essence of artistic experience is in the "aesthetic experience as qualitative experience," and the methodological principle creating artistic experience from experience is in the "expression of qualities of experience through the construction of qualitative materials." To achieve continuity from the experience of occupations to artistic experience, it is important to focus on the qualities of experience. So what are they?

1. The qualities of experience

Dewey stated that when occupations are viewed as experience, they are technical and aesthetic. Activities are divided between those intended for industry and those for art by whether they attempt to achieve some kind of usefulness or a direct quality that appeal to people's preferences (*MW*9: 246). A "direct quality" here refers to "all qualities directly had" rather than mediated through linguistic symbols, meaning that direct qualities that appeal to preferences and provide enjoyment are aesthetic quality (*LW*1: 90-91). When someone controls this directly experienced quality as value through interaction with materials, art is born.

Dewey noted that "All direct experience is qualitative, and qualities are what make life-experience itself directly precious" (*LW*10: 297), revealing that we live in a qualitative world and being qualitative is meaningful. Elsewhere he documented that "Those who are called artists have for their subject-matter the qualities of things of direct experience; 'intellectual' inquirers deal with these qualities at one remove, through the medium of symbols" (LW10: 80), saying that compared with scientists, who handle "qualities" indirectly through symbols, artists are distinguished by handling them directly. The experience of occupation is focused around direct experience through the physical senses. Qualities permeating the situation exist there, among which the qualities of things are fully experienced. That is, the qualities of experience can be said to be the qualities of things/situation sensed through direct experience. These qualities serve as resources for artistic experience.

2. Continuity from occupations to artistic experience

Next, let us consider how the qualities experienced through occupations lead to artistic experience. To lead with the conclusion, the connection between occupations and artistic experience is that the qualities experienced through occupations become artistic experience when expressed with qualitative materials. In other words, the continuity between life-experience and artistic experience is in the experience of qualities. Below is a more detailed discussion.

(1) The experience of qualities

Dewey stated that the world of direct experience is "the world of immediate experience in which art operates" (LW10: 341), considering art to be characterized by its use of the qualities of things directly experienced as subject-matter (LW10: 80). The qualities of things are experienced not individually but in fusion with the qualities of the situation interacting therewith.

What are the qualities of a situation? Dewey used "situation" to refer to the space where people and their environment interplay (LW13: 24). We do not experience things or events separately but within a contextual whole. A "situation" is this contextual whole (LW12: 72). The situation is unified as a coherent whole by the qualities with which it is permeated. These permeated qualities meld all the elements of the experience's interactions, endowing the situation with coherent wholeness and making it unique as well (*LW*12: 73–74). The qualities permeating the situation as a whole are the qualities of the situation.

They are imbued with the qualities of things experienced. For instance, in the occupation of weaving, children find when carding raw sheep wool that it has a scratchy texture. This is the sensory quality of the thing in question (raw wool). The qualities of things of this kind are not discrete individual matters but involved with the qualities of the various elements making up the situation. These include the various sensations acquired through experience such as the past sensation of touching a sheep at a farm, the sense of the hands' motion when carding wool into yarn, and so on. Given Dewey's point that "[t]he undefined pervasive quality of an experience is that which binds together all the defined elements, the objects of which we are focally aware, making them a whole" (*LW*10: 198), the qualities of a situation are thought to be created when the qualities of its elements and components meld together. Therefore, the qualities of a situation are imbued with the sensory qualities of the various things constituting the experience. When attention is focused consciously on the act of "carding raw wool" therein, the sensory quality of scratchiness emerges and is remembered as the quality of the thing in question. In the direct experience of occupations, children interact with materials while experiencing the quality of a unified, integrated situation.

Qualities can be grasped only through the physical senses. Because occupations are founded on the "coordinated sensory-motor function," the qualities of a situation become especially easy to experience through the active workings of the senses in integration with the body and mind. The qualities experienced in occupations are not those of discrete individual things but integrated qualities melded with those of the situation. When the experience of these qualities is concentrated and expressed, it becomes art (*LW*10: 199). This suggests that the continuity between life-experience/experience in occupations and artistic experience is to be found in the experience of qualities.

(2) Expression through qualitative materials

To express the experience of qualities, expressive media is required. Qualitative media such as color, sound, or motion are employed. For example, children who are absorbed in flying kites experience the qualities of the situation thereof, but the activity of kite flying itself is still not an artistic experience. It becomes one when the qualities of the situation and things experienced there are expressed in inter-action with qualitative media such as color, sound, or motion. This is where the qualitative media are called for. Kite flying involves the experience of qualities such as the way the kites flutter across the sky. The quality of fluttering lightness here experienced becomes an artistic experience when expressed using qualitative media such as color, sound, or motion. Depending on the medium used, the result may be a dance, a piece of music, or a visual artwork. The experience of qualities in occupations develops into artistic experience through the attainment of qualitative expressive media.

(3) The significance of the experience of qualities in occupations

In what way is it significant to experience qualities in occupations? As Dewey stated, "[t]he material of the fine arts consists of qualities" (*LW*10: 45), as does that of artistic experience. In occupations, an attitude of play is demonstrated, enabling children to try interacting with various materials with free rein for their imagina-tions. Therefore, occupations enable plentiful experience of qualities through trying various things. Having the senses cooperate with the body and mind to experience plentiful qualities in occupations promises to lead to richer artistic expression.

At the same time, Dewey considered that the aspect of experiencing various qual-ities through interaction with materials of this kind in occupations functions to shape value standards for individual behavior. During the production and con-struction process of occupations, children select qualities that appeal to their tastes from the process of trying out ideas and notions freely. This selection is thought to create their own aesthetic value standards. Dewey mentioned that the fine arts subjects are significant in their formation of aesthetic value standards (*MW*9: 246-247). This relates to the raison d'être of the fine arts subjects as well.

Dewey held that when a specific quality experienced is perceived as pleasant, it is remembered within the self as a value, forming aesthetic value standards. Art is what happens when these aesthetic value standards work to concentrate and express the aesthetic quality scattered throughout life-experience. The capacity to find these scattered qualities therein constitutes the "organs of vision" (*MW*9: 247), and cultivating these organs will lead to acting so as to enhance the aesthetic quality of everyday experience.

3. Specific examples of the development from occupations to artistic experience

Let us consider how the development from occupations to artistic experience plays out in specific activities in the case of music.

Discussing the characteristics of music within the fine arts, Dewey identified them as taking the quality of sense and, "by use of formal relationships transform[ing] the material into the art that is most remote from practical preoccupations" (*LW*10: 243–244). That is, he considered music to be characterized by the more direct expression of the qualities of life experience purely as qualities. Here, let us consider how the qualities experienced in occupations are expressed as music to demonstrate the relations between music and life experience.

A specific example of this development is the occupation of weaving. In *The School and Society*, Dewey noted that products of the introduction into the workroom of the concept of "fine arts" may include the Scotch song at the wheel or the spinning songs of Marguerite and Wagner's Senta (*MW*1: 54). Spinning songs are folk songs created from the work of spinning yarn. The "Scotch song at the wheel" is an example from Scotland of the spinning songs found worldwide. This shows that the work of spinning wool was part of daily life worldwide.

Let us now consider how this work transmutes into "spinning songs." Spinning was originally a household task. We may imagine that people not only produced yarn as an industry but also experienced the qualities of spinning work. The production of yarn has practical value while also possessing the aesthetic value of the experience of the qualities of the work. As noted above, occupations are characterized by their integration of practical and artistic values.

The quality of the work of spinning may be thought to be as follows. In spinning, the spinning wheel rotates in linkage with the top-like spindle, which rotates faster as the yarn winds around it. When focusing on the quality of things created in this situation (a sense of whirling of the spindle) and finding it pleasant and interesting, the artistic desire or impulse toward an expression arises. The movement of this ordinary tool evokes various imageries. For example, people might have sensed the quality of the light, continuous rotation of the wheel, brought meaning to it with the image of a fleet-footed young girl dancing, and chosen to express this image in sound. Songs entitled "Spinning Song" are, in fact, often characterized by a rapid rhythm and a flowing melody, with repeating phrases like the revolving spindle (whether they are folk songs, Mendelssohn, or Wagner). Spinning songs like this can be seen as expressions in sound through the artistic instinct of the quality of situations and things in the work of spinning.

To develop occupations into artistic experience, it is essential first to direct children's attention to the quality of their experience, that is of things and situations. Moreover, the environment must be constituted to enable the children to exert their current capacity in the expression of the qualities experienced through qualitative media.

Notes

1. Dewey himself, unwilling to assign adjectives to experience, does not use the term "artistic experience." He refers to the experience of art or of the artist. Here these are expressed as "artistic experience."

2. Given that Dewey's term "expression" refers to the act of artistic experience, an interaction between active and passive, this includes not only the productive activity of playing an instrument but also the perceptive activity of music appreciation.

3. While there was some awareness of the connection to occupations in visual art, specialized techniques (perspective, proportion, spaces, masses, balance, and effect of color combinations or contrasts) were taught in expressive activities related to occupations (Mayhew & Edwards: 182).

Chapter

A Theory of Artistic Construction Activity Based on the Concept of Occupation

Based on the concept of occupation provided in Chapter 1, this chapter will use the understanding of artistic experience established in Chapter 2 to build a theory of "artistic construction activity." The development of artistic experience based on the concept of occupation enables anyone to have artistic experience at school. The method used in this development is "artistic construction activity." This chapter will clarify the essence and methodological principles of this activity and consider the process, psychological, and social aspects constituting its structure (See Table 1 at the end of this chapter).

Essence and methodological principles of artistic construction activity

Occupation, construction activity, and artistic construction activity

1. Occupation and construction activity

To date in Japan, occupation has been put to use as an educational method in "construction activity." Construction activity is a type of activity that finds significance in the human act of constructing materials in an occupation.

This concept was first introduced into Japanese music education in 2001. At the time, construction activity was seen as having the requirements of occupation: (1) based on instinct or impulse, (2) using the physical organs, (3) composed of continuous interactions with materials, (4) creating external results, and (5) creating communication (Kojima 2001: 175). In 2010, construction activity was defined as follows. Construction activity is "activity in a social situation, originating from impulse, which uses the physical organs to construct an inner world related to the construction of works in the outer world" (Kojima 2010: 2). This definition specifies the perspective of "inner and outer construction": along with the construction of things or works in the outer world, the child's interior world is likewise reconstructed.

2. The core of construction activity

Dewey described occupation as "expressive and constructive activity" (*MW*1: 318). In his terms, construction is expression of the self. Occupation in its primary sense is an "expression through the physical organs" (*MW*1: 92). Dewey added that its purpose lies "in the growth that comes from the continual interplay of ideas and their embodiment in action" (*MW*1: 92). Inner ideas are embodied (expressed) in outer actions and thus changed; this interplay between the inner and outer self enables children to grow. This growth is itself the purpose of occupation. "Doing" in occupation refers to connecting and constructing outer materials. "Constructing" means creating a single unified whole. By constructing outer materials, children's inner materials having to do with intellect, sensitivity, will, etc., are likewise reconstructed and integrated, attaining wholeness. Therefore, children are able to experience holistic growth through occupation.

As indicated by Dewey, the construction of outer things in occupation is not simply a mechanical process of making things, but an expression of inner thought, emotion, images, and will. Here the inner and outer selves are correlated, so that a change in the shape of the outer materials will likewise bring about change to the inner materials. This means that when outer materials are constructed, inner materials are likewise reconstructed in relation to them. In short, construction applies to both inner and outer materials. This is "the double construction of the inner and outer self" which lies at the core of construction activity.

Based thereupon, construction activity is a way of grasping occupation as an educational method employing the "double construction of the inner and outer self,"[1] and therefore cultivating children's interiority.

3. Construction activity and artistic construction activity

How is "construction activity" related to "artistic construction activity," the topic of this book?

Occupation is a form of activity which brings life experience into school education, structured so as to differentiate and develop undifferentiated and unified life experience into specialized experience of academic study, science, and cultural arts. Naturally, life experience must have an artistic aspect as well; however, as we saw in Chapter 2, no one at Dewey's Laboratory School had access to a methodology for developing occupation into artistic experience at the time.

As noted in Chapter 2, the essence of artistic experience is aesthetic experience handling qualitative materials for the purpose of aesthetic qualities, that is, "aesthetic experience as experience of qualities." The activity here uses qualitative materials such as color or sound to express the qualities of experience in the form of tangible artwork. When the materials worked on with body and mind in construction activity are qualitative materials composed of unique properties, the construction activity's content is that of artistic experience. This is "artistic construction activity."

In other words, construction activity constructs outer materials. When the outer materials are qualitative materials such as color, sound, movement, or light, the construction activity's content is that of artistic experience. This is "artistic construction activity." Construction activity focused on qualitative materials as the outer materials for construction is "artistic construction activity."

Essence and methodological principles of artistic construction activity

1. Essence of artistic construction activity

Where is the essence of artistic construction activity to be found?

We have concluded that the essence of occupation is "direct experience as life experience," and that the essence of artistic experience is "aesthetic experience as qualitative experience." How, then, does life experience develop into artistic experience as aesthetic experience? This is where the essence of artistic construction activity lies. This point is discussed in detail below.

What are the seeds of art in life experience? Dewey identified seeds of art in the zest of the spectator who pokes logs in the fireplace to see them collapse as the flame shoots up or in the pleasure of the housewife in tending her garden. He likewise found them in the artisan who handles his materials and tools with love, taking pains to create something better, more satisfactory. He considered aesthetic qualities to be found in the experience of happy absorption in the activities of mind and body (*LW*10: 10). Experiences leading to absorption are those in which all the elements of experience are integrated through impulse or interest, creating a unified whole from beginning to end — that is, "an experience." Dewey observed aesthetic qualities in the integrated, unified, harmonic movement which makes experience into "an experience." In his view, the situation of complete, pure integration between the object of attention and the mind is aesthetic.

In this way, we experience aesthetic qualities amid everyday experience; however, the experience at the time is not intended for taking pleasure in aesthetic qualities. The housewife absorbed in tending her garden is struck by the smell of the soil and the color and texture of the petals, enjoying this direct experience, but the purpose of her action is on the practical side of cultivating plants successfully. In contrast, there are also experiences in which we are interested in the direct qualities we enjoy amid everyday experience, where creating and savoring these qualities is the actual purpose. These experiences constitute artistic experience as aesthetic experience. The essence of artistic experience is the direct expression of the qualities of direct experience, through qualitative media such as color and sound, without using signs or symbols. If the housewife tending her plants were trying to express the qualities of the scent and softness of the soil and the vividness of the petals which she has experienced using qualitative media such as color or lines, this would be an artistic experience. In short, artistic experience is the experience of perceiving the qualities experienced in life and expressing them with qualitative media. Here we find the continuity from life experience to artistic experience. Thus, life experience and artistic experience can be grasped as continuous in terms of the experience of qualities.

In sum, artistic construction activity is a perspective on artistic experience from the concept of occupation as an educational method, as well as a mode of activity intended to develop the seeds of art latent in life experience into artistic experience. Therefore, the essence of artistic construction activity can be found in "continuity from life experience to artistic experience through the perception of qualities."

2. Methodological principles of artistic construction activity

The essence of artistic construction activity is "continuity from life experience to artistic experience through the perception of qualities." It is a mode of activity intended to develop life experience continuously into artistic experience. What methodological principles can artistic construction activity adopt in order to realize this essence?

In Chapter 2, we found that the methodological principle for making experience artistic was "expression of the qualities of experience through the construction of qualitative materials," or direct expression of the qualities of direct experience through qualitative media such as color or sound. The qualities of direct experience are those experienced in everyday life. Life experience can be made continuous with artistic experience by focusing on the qualities of this life experience. Children are asked to do so and to express these qualities through qualitative media. Thus, we may say that the methodological principle of artistic construction activity is the "expression of the qualities of life experience through the construction of qualitative materials."

Generally, the junction or continuity of life and art requires a continuity of subject. One example of this is writing or singing Christmas carols at Christmastime. This act may have the potential to become artistic experience continuous with life. However, a condition applies: the artistic experience must take place in a form continuous with the children's life experience. It is a misconception to think that singing Christmas carols is related to the life experience of Christmas. Often, the connection between them is no more than the word "Christmas." The child's inner self — how they experience Christmas, and what parts of the experience they were struck by — must be considered. The construction of the environment which expresses the qualities of the Christmas situation experienced by the child — waking in the morning to find wrapped and beribboned presents, the excitement of opening them, the glitter of the gold ribbon — gives rise to the unique qualitative situation of the Christmas experience of *that child*. It is this qualitative aspect of life experience that creates the continuity between life experience and artistic experience.

That is, for artistic experience to retain continuity with life experience, the activity must be realized as "the expression of the qualities of life experience through the construction of qualitative materials." How can that be achieved? By directing children's attention to the qualitative aspect of experience and leading them to perceive these qualities. The qualitative aspect of experience refers to the qualities of situations and the qualities of things embedded therein. It is the experience of qualities that creates continuity between everyday life experience and art. In artistic construction activity developing life experience into artistic experience, children's attention must be drawn to the qualitative aspect of their experiences. In addition, the environment must be constructed so as to have them express these experiences in qualitative media such as color and sound.

In sum, the methodological principles of artistic construction activity are "the expression of the qualities of life experience through the construction of qualitative materials," and the construction of an environment which enables children to experience the expression of the qualities experienced in life through qualitative materials in artistic construction activity.

Structure of artistic construction activity

Next, let us clarify the structure of artistic construction activity through the process, psychological, and social aspects. Occupation is an intentional educative experience promoting children's growth. Artistic construction activity based on the concept of occupation is a method for deliberately making artistic experience into educative experience. From this perspective, through discussing the three aspects of occupation and artistic experience previously examined (process, psychological, and social), this section considers the fundamental points and elements of each aspect of artistic construction activity.

The process aspect

1. Fundamental point and elements

(1) Fundamental point

The process aspect of artistic construction activity is a chronological view of the interaction of children and materials: the aspect in which the activity develops from beginning to end. The fundamental point of the process aspect is that, as with occupation and artistic experience, this is "an experience" where meaning is accumulated from beginning through development to end. "An experience" is developed as "inquiry" in occupation and "expression" in artistic experience.

In artistic construction activity, "expression" is developed as "inquiry." This is in order to render artistic experience an intentional "educative experience." According to Dewey, the process of inquiry is thinking itself (*MW*9: 155), and inquiry is "the method of an educative experience" (*MW*9: 170). Experience is reconstructed as the children themselves become the subjects of the activity, thinking and transforming the situation: this is where growth occurs. To this end, it is effective to organize the artistic construction activity aimed at children's growth as the process of inquiry. However, this inquiry, unlike that of occupation, is inquiry as "expression," that is, "artistic inquiry."[2] Based on the above, the fundamental point of the process aspect of artistic construction activity is "'an experience' as artistic inquiry."

(2) Elements

To realize "'an experience' as artistic inquiry," the interaction between children and materials must involve "expression," following the process of "inquiry." The elements required for this are presented below. First, there is "impulsion and resistance," second, "creative problem-solving as inquiry," and third, "sharing of artworks as products." Below is a more detailed discussion of each element.

2. Discussion of elements

(1) Impulsion and resistance

Inquiry begins with an "uncertain situation" in which the balance between the environment and the organism has broken down. This is equivalent to the situation in which impulsion encounters resistance and expression begins. "An experience" in artistic construction activity begins with an environment likely to evoke children's impulsion. Therefore, it is a given that children act upon the materials of the environment not based on someone's instructions but through the impulse and interest welling up within themselves. The stimulation of impulsion serves as the beginning of "an experience."

The stimulated impulsion must then encounter resistance in order to find a direction. Resistance creates an "uncertain situation"; the children become confused and register the situation as a "problem situation," reflect on how to recover its stability, and work to solve the problem. Resistance is a condition for getting inquiry started, or in other words, for bringing about reflective thinking.

What does resistance consist of in artistic construction activity? Resistance is not something brought into the activity from outside the situation; rather, it is found within the impulsive activity in progress. Through its place in the context of the children's own activity as their impulsion functions, resistance is capable of evoking reflection in the children; likewise, hints for overcoming resistance are not far to seek, being found within the situation in progress.

For example, children may enjoy dangling various metal bowls used for cooking and striking them to hear them reverberate. This is a "certain situation" in which the children are exerting impulsion and becoming absorbed in their activity, in harmony with the situation. Here the teacher suggests choosing an order to strike the bowls in, making up a pattern and repeating it (a technique called "ostinato"). This ostinato suggestion functions as resistance for the children, who are simply enjoying hitting the bowls, and evokes reflection. Choosing to strike the bowls in a given order creates a sound pattern, such as "ding-dong-deng-ding". While the children were previously striking the bowls at random, uninterested in the order of the sounds, they act differently once they have gained the purpose of creating a pattern to strike in. They try various orders to find out which process of sound pleases them. Through this act of selection, the thoughts and feelings of the self are made conscious: "I think this is a good sound pattern," "This pattern of sounds makes me feel sad somehow," and so on, finding a direction for the activity.

Resistance for the children here is the ostinato technique. The ostinato is a basic technique of repeating a pattern, which has been used across time and place when humanity organizes sounds and shapes them into music. The ostinato is a product of human inquiry, a material of culture (constructing culture). Here, a material of musical culture has been used as resistance for impulsion.

As this example shows, resistance does not obstruct impulsion; it creates a moment of pause, and it develops the impulsive activity toward its next step. The ostinato as resistance is conceived by the teacher *within the situation* in which children are absorbed in striking bowls. If the teacher were to bring in a task of some kind from the outside as resistance, it would create a context unrelated to the children's impulsion, and fail to serve as resistance for them. The nature of the resistance must be identified within the original "certain situation" in which the children are absorbed in activity.

(2) Creative problem-solving as inquiry

Through encountering resistance, children enter an "uncertain situation," and begin problem-solving in order to recover the "certain situation." In occupation, the problem-solving is guided by logic; in artistic inquiry, the guide is "images."

In artistic inquiry, the sense of disharmony between inner materials (images, etc.) and outer materials (color, sound, etc.) is the "uncertain situation," or the problematic situation. Children observe the problem situation in order to find the cause and resolve the sense of disharmony. They listen to the music, observe its status, and acquire ideas like "the music doesn't sound unified, so what if I make the end gradually louder so it sounds grander." They manipulate and experiment with the sounds, making them louder in order to express grandeur. This sense of grandeur is an image of the qualities of things previously experienced by the child in question. As the inner and outer materials are thus harmonized and unified through the interaction of "doing" and "undergoing," problem-solving in artistic inquiry takes place. This form of problem-solving differs from scientific inquiry in that images rather than logic take the lead.

Further, in the problem-solving of artistic inquiry, children's search for a resolution is not linear. Children make detours, trying various potential expressions with the materials, and thus enjoying the process of experiencing new qualities in itself. This is what Dewey referred to as the cultivation of resistance, putting off problem-solving rather than attempting to get it out of the way immediately when encountering resistance and recognizing a problem situation (*LW*10: 21). When a certain idea arises within the problem situation, new facts come to light through experimenting with the idea. The inquirer is stimulated by these new facts to come up with more new ideas. This shows that artistic inquiry is not, like scientific inquiry, a process of finding a single solution for a problem, but a form of creative problem-solving finding meaning in the ideas gained through experimentation with various solutions.

(3) Sharing of artworks as products

When the "certain situation" is recovered through the interaction with materials, "an experience" is consummated in the creation of a product.

The products of occupations are those created with the addition of human manipulation to the substances of the natural world. They are an embodiment of the cumulative meaning of the process. In occupation, this meaning is the generalized meaning of the connections among social and scientific phenomena. Therefore, the meaning of the products can be separated from the process and used independently in a new situation, serving as a tool to expand and deepen the next experience.

By contrast, the products of artistic experience are the artworks created with the addition of human manipulation to the qualities of the natural world. In artistic experience, because the materials are qualitative, the products are expressions of qualitative meaning. Qualitative meaning is accumulated by unifying the partial qualities into a whole, so that the final product takes the meaning of a unified whole. Therefore, the product is meaningless if separated from the process.

The products of artistic construction activity, like artistic experience, are artworks. Further, the important point of artistic inquiry is that as a result of interaction with materials, the environment and the self are integrated, satisfying the inner self in terms of impulse, interest, emotion, etc. Therefore, the works which are the final products of artistic construction activity cannot be positively or negatively compared with the works of others: they are valuable in their individuality as expressions of the self.

Further, in artistic construction activity, as in occupation, expressive activity is conducted as a joint activity with a common end, because communication among multiple children is expected to be educationally effective. Here, sharing works with others is important. At the end of "an experience" in artistic construction activity, just as the individual's impulses and emotions are embodied in an artwork, the work is given significance through being shared with others.

The psychological aspect of artistic construction activity

1. Fundamental point and elements

(1) Fundamental point

The psychological aspect of artistic construction activity relates to how children interact with materials. In artistic construction activity, as in occupation and artistic experience, interactions are psychosomatic. Psychosomatic interactions are carried out as interactions between inner and outer materials. However, the outer materials differ between occupation and artistic experience: Occupation uses social materials, while artistic experience uses qualitative materials. The difference in materials means that the interactions are furthered by logical thinking in occupation, and by qualitative thinking in artistic experience. In artistic construction activity, which contains artistic experience, interactions are essentially qualitative thinking. Therefore, the fundamental point of artistic construction activity, as with artistic experience, is "qualitative thinking through the psychosomatic interaction."

(2) Elements

Qualitative thinking through the psychosomatic interaction is carried out in expression as "the interaction of inner and outer (qualitative) materials." The first element, therefore, is the interaction of inner and outer (qualitative) materials. To carry out this interaction, the materials which serve as the target of impulsion are first required. Upon acquiring the materials, the children work upon them and are worked upon in turn. That is, the active "doing" and passive "undergoing" become connected.

When the interaction of inner and outer (qualitative) materials is grasped as the connections between "doing" and "undergoing," reflective thinking takes place within this interaction. Reflective thinking in artistic construction activity is qualitative, grasping the connections between "doing" and "undergoing" directly and qualitatively rather than in terms of logical cause and effect. Based on this, the second element is the perception of the qualitative relationship between "doing" and "undergoing."

Artists create their works through this perception; however, in the case of children, not everyone can easily achieve it. Even so, the perception of the qualitative connections between "doing" and "undergoing" is the key to children's growth. Artistic construction activity is important in that it leads children carefully through the process of "inquiry" to evoke this perception. Artistic construction activity works to circulate the cycle of "observation – end-in-view – experiment," centered on images.

This cycle can be described as follows. Children manipulate outer materials, change their forms, and observe the results, acquiring some kind of image of their target. Next, in order to realize the image, they form an "end-in-view" and experiment on it. Experimentation here refers to manipulating and changing the form of outer materials. Inner and outer materials continuously interact through the cycle of observing, acquiring an end-in-view from observation, experimenting. The third element, therefore, is the "circulation of the cycle of 'observation – end-in-view – experiment' centered on images." The circulation of this cycle is the core point which renders artistic construction activity an educative experience through which children grow.

The basis of this cycle, as with occupation, is thought to lie in the multilayered thought structure of "body, image, and reflection." Experimentation is mainly equivalent to the body, observation to the image, and end-in-view to the reflection. Therefore, the circulation of the cycle of "observation – end-in-view – experiment" indicates it is simultaneously carried out in the dimensions of the modes of thought involving body, image, and reflection. This multilayered thought structure (body, image, reflection) renders psychosomatic interaction possible. The fourth element, then, is "the multilayered thought structure of 'body, image, and reflection'."

Below is a more detailed discussion of each element.

2. Discussion of elements

(1) Interaction of inner and outer (qualitative) materials

Because artistic construction activity contains artistic experience, it involves the interaction of inner and outer (qualitative) materials. This interaction requires inner and outer materials as a premise. Inner materials belong to the inner world of the child, such as impulse, images, concepts, thoughts, emotions, memories, etc. Outer materials are qualitative materials which can be perceived objectively, for example with sight or hearing. In the case of music, they are sounds, elements of musical composition (rhythm, melody, timbre, tempo, etc.), form, technique, rendition, etc.

The energy linking these inner and outer materials is interest. Interest is based on life experience. The outer materials of occupation are social materials. Viewed psychologically, these social materials are basically the materials familiar in daily life. The materials of the everyday environment have in their favor that they con-stitute a background network of significance for children, making it easier for the children to find connections with themselves and to develop interest. Therefore, in artistic construction activity as well, the materials to be found ought not to be specialized abstract elements or techniques but those within children's life experience in order to pique their interest. At the same time, the materials of life experience are well known to the children. The outer materials must enable free and unlimited handling, like an extension of the children's own bodies, for interaction to occur. This suggests that to enable interaction among inner and outer materials in artistic construction activity, it is effective to draw both inner and outer materials from life experience.

(2) Perception of the qualitative connections between "doing" and "undergoing"

Next, to achieve continuous interaction between inner and outer materials, the children must perceive intellectually the connections between "doing" and "undergoing." The same applies in occupation and in artistic experience. In occupation, however, the logical connections between "doing" and "undergoing" is perceived through logical thinking. In contrast, in artistic experience, which handles qualitative materials, the issue is the qualitative connections between "doing" and "undergoing" in interactions. For example, in the case of music, when the element of sound, an outer material, is changed ("doing"), the quality of the immediate situation changes, and this change is intuited through the senses ("undergoing"). The perception of the qualitative connections between "doing" and "undergoing" generates meaning which determines and gives direction to the next step of "doing." This qualitative connections, which gives direction to the next action, is qualitative thinking. In artistic construction activity, as in artistic experience, qualitative thinking perceives the qualitative connections between "doing" and "undergoing."

(3) Circulation of the cycle of "observation – end-in-view – experiment" centered on images

What thinking methods should children adopt to carry out the qualitative thinking above?

In artistic inquiry, the connection between "doing" and "undergoing" is carried out as the cycle of "observation – end-in-view – experiment," as detailed below. Artistic inquiry is characterized by having images at the center of this cycle. As noted above, the cycle's circulation is at the core of artistic construction activity.

Formation of images through observation of facts. In artistic inquiry, the products created in the outer world through the interaction of inner and outer materials are the "facts" of the situation. Children "observe" the facts that have thus come to light. In artistic inquiry, observation uses the perceptual methods of "sensing and feeling." "Sensing" in this case means perceiving the structure of the target as a fact through the physical senses, and "feeling" means intuiting the qualities that permeate the target. Because these two operations take place simultaneously and in relation to each other, albeit remaining undivided, the qualitative connections between "doing" and "undergoing" is perceived.

"Doing" and "undergoing" in artistic inquiry are connected and endowed with meaning by the image formed through sensing and feeling. Consider this example. When children playing music add in dynamics, the music acting as the target of the interaction in the situation changes, as do the qualities permeating the entire situation. Changing the dynamics turns a previously static quality into a fluctuating one. By feeling this changed quality, similar experiences in the past are evoked, and their meanings become part of the current experience. The sense of fluctuation is comparable to the feeling of the waves on a beach that the children visited in the past. Here it is "imagination" which connects past and present experience. Children make use of their imagination to grasp the qualities generated by the current situation with the image of fluctuating waves in their past experience. This "feeling of wavelike fluctuation" becomes the meaning of that piece of music. Next, they "consciously" make sounds which suit the image of the fluctuating waves. The acquisition of meaning changes the approach to the target. Thereafter, the quality of the music changes, and the image is revised again. In this perception of qualities, past and present experiences are linked by imagination, forming an image which becomes the meaning of the music. The image gives meaning to the qualitative relationship.

Thus, when the qualitative relationship between "doing" and "undergoing" is perceived through the methods of sensing and feeling, an image is formed from the perception of qualities and brings meaning to the product (artwork) as fact. "Doing" and "undergoing" are linked by images, creating meaning.

Formation of end-in-view. With their sense perceptions of facts as materials, children next form an end-in-view.

End-in-view refers to a potentially achievable end which is brought to mind in order to solve the problem created within the currently ongoing activity. This is not a far-distant goal, but an end with an achievable method built in: "This should do it." Further, given that this is sometimes called "the foreseen and desired end" (*MW*9: 134), it must be an end which foresees the conclusion of the activity, and one whose realization is desired by the doers themselves.

Dewey considered the end-in-view as a manifestation of children's interest. When children foresee during an activity that "if I do this, this will happen," and desire to "do it this way next," that is, when they have an end-in-view, there is interest (*MW*9: 134). In practice, the "end-in-view" takes the important role of manipulating situations to the next step, bearing interest with it. The role of the end-in-view is to render interaction continuous.

The end-in-view can create continuity among experiences because it is both the ends and the means of the activity. According to Dewey, "an end [end-in-view] which grows up within an activity as plan for its direction is always both ends and means. Every means is a temporary end until we have attained it. Every end becomes a means of carrying activity further as soon as it is achieved" (*MW*9: 113). When children achieve their end, it becomes a means toward a new end. By combining the functions of the end and the means, the end-in-view guarantees continuity of interaction.

In the process of replacing the end and means while advancing the activity, the end-in-view can also be considered a hypothesis to be tested and verified through the activity. Dewey noted that "[t]he aim[end-in-view], in short, is experimental, and hence constantly growing as it is tested in action" (*MW*9: 112). Therefore, the generation of the end-in-view enables continuity in the interactions with the environment over repeated experiments. The end-in-view can be considered an important concept which forms the core of realizing continuity of experience within the practice of artistic construction activity.

Experiments. When children have an end-in-view, they put it into practice. This can be called an "experiment." As noted above, the end-in-view is experimental.

Here, let us consider "experiments" in Dewey's terms. For Dewey, experiments are not limited to what scientists conduct in laboratories, but involve basic human methods of perception (*MW*9: 280). These methods refer to the essence of experience: the perception of things by discovering the relationship between "doing" and "undergoing." Experience contains active and passive elements: on the active side it is *trying*, and on the passive side it is *undergoing* (*MW*9: 146). "Trying" in this sense means experimenting.

For artistic construction activity to become an educative experience rather than simply an activity, the children must "learn from experience." According to Dewey, "[t]o 'learn from experience' is to make a backward and forward connection between what we do to things and what we enjoy or suffer from things in consequence. Under such conditions, doing becomes a trying" (*MW*9: 147). This means that the children are doing "an experiment with the world" (*MW*9: 147). The term "experiment" serves as a single word expressing "psychosomatic interactions" from the dimension of practice.

Dewey's "experiments," as presented above, include not only those with an end-in-view possessed of clear foresight but also trial-and-error experiments that "test out" suggestions. Artistic construction activity does not consist of thinking up a melody and then writing notes on staff paper. It is an activity in which children interact directly with qualitative materials, or in other words, experiment while creating artwork. This requires an "attitude of play." Interactions derived from an attitude of play result in trial-and-error such as "just wanting to try and see what happens," which is where the fundamental significance of artistic construction activity lies. This significance is the chance to experience plentiful qualities. It is through the trial-and-error process of trying one thing and then another that children can experience various qualities. While they may not be immediately embodied in artwork, the experiences of these qualities are accumulated in the subconscious. Through the provision of sufficient time and space for trial-and-error experiments, children can accumulate sufficient experience of qualities, and when this subconscious accumulation is revived in other situations later on, they can develop new images and ideas.

In short, sufficient trial-and-error experiments are important in artistic construction activity, and based on these experiments, it becomes possible to conduct experimentation with the end-in-view as a hypothesis.

The cycle of "observation – end-in-view – experiment" centered on images.
Let us summarize the circulation of the cycle of "observation – end-in-view – experiment" centered on images, as discussed above. Children observe the facts resulting from what they have done via the perceptual methods of sensing and feeling. Here the qualities of the facts are perceived via the medium of images. To express these images, they form an end-in-view and experiment with it. They then observe the facts which appear as the result of the experiment, revise their images, and update their end-in-view. The circulation of this cycle promotes qualitative thinking.

In artistic construction activity, building an environment that enables the cycle of "observation – end-in-view – experiment" to circulate, with images at its center, connects "doing" and "undergoing" and furthers psychosomatic interactions. As the circulation of the cycle unifies inner and outer materials into a whole, a satisfactory artwork is created as the conclusion.

(4) The multilayered thought structure of "body, image, and reflection"

The "observation – end-in-view – experiment" cycle centering on images in artistic construction activity is a method for realizing qualitative thinking. As with occupation, a multilayered thought structure of "body, image, and reflection" is arranged within.

"Experiments" are based on forms of thought in the physical dimension. Observation through sensing and feeling facts as the results of experiments means perceiving the qualities experienced from the facts present through the medium of each individual's free images. The form of thought of free representation is relevant here. When forming an end-in-view with the results of observation and perception as materials, the thought form of reflection, taking into account methods for achieving the end, is also relevant.

The foundation of artistic construction activity, which promotes the interaction of inner and outer materials through the circulation of the "observation – end-in-view – experiment" cycle centered on images, is the multilayered thought structure of "body, image, and reflection." This thought structure enables qualitative thinking via interaction.

The social aspect of artistic construction activity

1. Fundamental point and elements

(1) Fundamental point

The social aspect of artistic construction activity addresses how children are involved with others in the situation of interacting with materials

The fundamental point of this social aspect, as with occupation and artistic experience, is communication as the sharing of experience. In occupation, as a shared activity with a common end, individual experiences are exchanged, and the meaning of experiences is shared. Artistic experience involves the communication of qualities, as the producer and perceiver share the qualitative meaning of experience with the artwork as a medium. Through the work, the two recreate their experiences, sharing the qualitative meaning latent in the depths of life experience.

In artistic construction activity, because the shared experience is artistic, the main communication is that of the qualities of experience. The fundamental point of the social aspect of artistic construction activity, as with artistic experience, is "communication of quality as the sharing of experience."

(2) Elements

The first element required to realize "communication of quality as the sharing of experience" is "communication of quality in shared activities." Because artistic construction activity is an "educative experience" intended to enable children to exchange experiences and thus to grow, it involves, like occupation, shared activities with a common end. In these activities, the communication of qualities is conducted through the exchange of various qualitative experiences. The communication of quality is realized as the sharing of images of shared objects in shared activities. This gives rise to the second element, "formation of empathetic attitudes and community through the sharing of images." As images cannot be transmitted via language, a willingness to attempt to infer the other person's experience of qualities is required. This is the empathetic attitude of walking in the other person's shoes. Sharing images with an empathetic attitude creates a feeling of coexistence in the children taking part in the activity, leading to the formation of a community. Below is a more detailed discussion of each element.

2. Discussion of elements

(1) Communication of quality in shared activities

Shared activities. From an educational point of view, the important facet of "communication of qualities as the sharing of experience" is the reconstruction of experience on both ends of the communication in question, enabling both sender and receiver to grow. To bring this about, in artistic construction activity as in occupation, multiple children associate together in a collaborative shared activity with a common end.

To establish shared activity, *a shared object* mediating among multiple children is required. In the case of artistic construction activity, the shared object is the product as a work of art that externally expresses the quality or image percepted by individuals in sound, physical movement, color, shape, etc. This begins in fragmentary form and ends in construction as a unified work. Therefore, in shared activities, the end is to make the shared object into a work all group members are satisfied with, via communication among the group members concerning the shared object.

Communication of quality. In the exchange of experiences in artistic construction activity, communication of qualities is central, given that the shared object in shared activity is a product made with qualitative materials.

The prerequisite for communication with the product (artwork) as a medium in artistic experience is that the outer materials are not unknown and extraordinary, but rather common materials that exist in society. Because the individual's inner world where the materials are combined also exists within the social context, the inner materials can also be considered common (*LW*10: 54). Therefore, the artwork belongs to the public world and as such should be perceivable to others. If art is communication, then expression may be understood as the activity of transforming common materials through the exertion of the self, reissuing them to the public world. In addition, seen from the positioning of impulse in occupation, the social impulse of wanting to tell people something is at work, evoking the expressive impulse. In artistic construction activity as well, children use expression not simply for their own comfort but in order to construct works to be shared with others.

In artistic construction activity, as in occupation, communication mediated through products is more likely to occur when the inner and outer materials are familiar from life experience. One example of the practice of artistic construction activity involved a group creating music for sparklers. The group brought in outer materials with which they had enjoyed making noise in everyday life, such as plastic bags and wind chimes. The sound of the plastic bags was used to express the image (inner material) of sparks crackling off the sparklers. Most of the children in the class had experienced sparklers and enjoyed the crackling noise of the bags; each child enjoyed the music and verbally expressed their appreciation with each other. In artistic construction activity, the sharing of qualitative experience is easily achieved, because materials from life experience can be seen as cultural materials shared throughout the region or group.

Based on the above, in artistic construction activity, "common" materials are materials from "life experience." The producer transforms familiar materials from everyday life into a new substance, making use of their own intelligence and sensibility, and the perceiver likewise perceives the work by reconstructing familiar materials into new things in the same way. In Chapter 2, we saw that artistic experience makes it possible to sense in concentrated form the qualities located in the depths of everyday existence. Artistic construction activity has the same aim: to concentrate and experience the qualitative meanings located in the depths of life experience.

Sharing images. Because qualities are perceived through images, the communication of qualities is carried out as "sharing images" with regard to the shared object.

The use of multiple media in communication is an effective way to share images. Because the sender uses diverse qualitative media (sound, color, physical movement, etc.) as needed to represent images during the creative process, the perceivers themselves are able to perceive qualities and to deepen and expand their sensations. At the same time, the receivers use their own superior sense to perceive these qualities. In activities aimed at musical expression as well, for multiple children to share images in shared activities, they must repeatedly represent their own images with various qualitative media other than sound during the course of the activity. When representing images with sound is difficult, representation can be done easily with physical expression. Through physical representation, the child acquires a clearer sense of their own image, and the observers likewise come to understand: "Oh, okay, that's what you mean."

At the same time, verbal communication plays a major role in artistic construction activity, unlike artistic experience which does not require language. This is because artistic construction activity is a form of inquiry intended to promote children's growth. Reflective thinking is where inquiry comes into practice. In artistic construction activity, reflective thinking is qualitative; reflection is enabled by "intelligence." The intelligence connects doing and undergoing. The intelligence is consciousness, and consciousness requires language. Language is an effective way to perceive the qualitative relationship between doing and undergoing in the interaction of inner and outer materials within artistic construction activity. It is also effective for the communication of qualities with others. When creating a space for presentation as well, along with listening to one another's performances, conveying the performers' intent and ideas in words can assist the listeners in imagining the experience of the performers as others.

However, in all contexts, verbal communication must be treated as auxiliary to communication via qualitative media such as sound, color, or movement. Qualitative experiences cannot be shared via language alone. Language used to support and supplement communication via multiple media makes it easier for children to perceive the qualitative relationships of the artwork, the shared object, contributing to enable the sharing of images.

(2) Formation of empathetic attitudes and community through the sharing of images

To share images in artistic construction activity, the children must adopt empathetic attitudes.

For all we say "sharing" images, the sender and receiver do not have the exact same images in mind. Anything which can be conveyed to anyone in exactly the same way is not an image to begin with. The sharing of images, like the communication of the producer and perceiver mediated by artwork, is the communication of qualities. In the communication of qualities, information is not involved in the form of symbols. If children cannot focus with all their senses on the work presented by others, they will receive no information. The desire to listen, the will to hear are essential. The children present must each be willing to concentrate all their senses on receiving the information, *trying* to imagine the image held by the producer. The qualities thus sensed through the image will then influence the image of the work held by the listeners, expanding and deepening it. This is the communication of qualities.

In occupation, participation in a shared activity socially intellectualizes individual impulse and cultivates an attitude of empathy toward others. The conditions for shared activities include a common goal, interest in seeing it completed, and the coordination of individual actions with an eye to the common end. When taking part in shared activities, we are called on to imagine others' experience and walk in their shoes in order to grasp this stance at the root of experience. This is an empathetic attitude.

In artistic construction activity, the "common end" which is a condition for shared activity is intimately related to the sharing of images. This is because in the experience of artistic inquiry, images drive interaction, and ends arise based on images. As images cannot be conveyed in language, the sharing of images is impossible without an empathetic attitude disposed to imagine the experiences of others. In artistic construction activity, an empathetic attitude is even more urgently needed to enable the aim of shared images. Therefore, this activity can help to cultivate an empathetic attitude. Sharing images is expected to deepen individual perception while at the same time cultivating an attitude of concern and empathy for others.

However, it goes without saying that various problems arise during the process of sharing images. Planning artistic construction activity as shared activity involves creating a situation where connections among people exist, which is to say a social situation. Social situations involve clashing with others whose images and ideas differ. This is, in a sense, an uncertain situation. However, uncertain situations involve the potential for inquiry to begin as a way of resolving the uncertainty. This is social inquiry. In social inquiry, certain situations lead to the unity of the self with others. This enables not only the individual fulfillment of having completed a satisfactory work of art, but at the same time, the sense of continuity between the experience of the self and that of others, including the process of discussion in which diverse opinions are worked out. Because this continuity comes through the communication of qualities, it makes it possible to enjoy the feeling of coexistence, the sense of the self existing in company with others. This feeling of coexistence harbors the potential to make the class into a community.

Notes

1. "Constructive activity" as used in Dewey's writings refers to one out of multiple types of activities. "Construction activity" as used here refers to a mode of activity as an educational method.

2. In his theory of inquiry, Dewey discusses inquiry as the transformation of situations of experience, defining it as *"the controlled or directed transformation of an indeterminate situation into one that is so determinate in its constituent distinctions and relations as to convert the elements of the original situation into a unified whole"* (*LW*12: 108). Dewey's theory of inquiry refers to general, scientific, or social inquiry; no reference has been found to artistic inquiry. "Artistic inquiry" in this book discusses the author's application of Dewey's theory of inquiry to artistic experience.

Table 1. Connection of Occupation, Artistic Experience, and Artistic Construction Activity

		Occupation	Artistic experience	Artistic construction activity
Essence		Direct experience as life experience	Aesthetic experience as qualitative experience	Continuity from life experience to artistic experience through the perception of qualities
Methodological principle		Self-expression through the construction of materials	Expression of the qualities of experience through the construction of qualitative materials	Expression of the qualities of life experience through the construction of qualitative materials
Structure	Process aspect	"An experience" as inquiry	"An experience" as expression	"An experience"as artistic inquiry
		Impulse and interest Logical problem-solving as inquiry Products as outcomes	Impulsion and resistance Establish of expression Artworks as products	Impulsion and resistance Creative problem-solving as inquiry Sharing of artworks as products
	Psychological aspect	Logical thinking through the psychosomatic interaction	Qualitative thinking through the psychosomatic interaction	Qualitative thinking through the psychosomatic interaction
		Interaction of inner and outer materials Perception of the logical connections between "doing" and "undergoing" Multilayered thought structure of "body, image, and reflection"	Interaction of inner and outer (qualitative) materials Perception of the qualitative connections between "doing" and "undergoing" Expression of qualitative meaning	Interaction of inner and outer (qualitative)materials Perception of the qualitative connections between "doing" and "undergoing" Circulation of the cycle of "observation–end-in-view–experiment" centered on images Multilayered thought structure of "body, image, and reflection"
	Social aspect	Communication as the sharing of experience	Communication of quality as the sharing of experience	Communication of quality as the sharing of experience
		Communication in shared activities Socialization of impulse and formation of empathetic attitude	Communication of quality between producer and perceiver with public artworks as the medium Formation of publicness through sharing qualities of the public world	Communication of quality in shared activities Formation of empathetic attitudes and community through the sharing of images

An Activity Model and Practice of Artistic Construction Activity

Chapter 3 formulated a theory of artistic construction activity. How, then, can this activity be embodied in practice? This chapter presents an activity model that serves as hints for this embodiment in practice, from the perspective of how the teacher should build the learning environment. Next, it offers examples of specific practice for the activity model.

An activity model for artistic construction activity

Activity model Table

An activity model for artistic construction activity is shown in Table 2. Below is an explanation of how this activity model has been derived from the theory of artistic construction activity.

First, the fundamental points of the process, psychological, and social aspects of artistic construction activity, as deduced in Chapter 3, and the elements required to realize them were confirmed. In other words, these elements are "criteria" that artistic construction activity must meet. Artistic construction activity was thus defined as activity meeting these criteria.

Next, the perspectives required to build a learning environment that meets the criteria for each aspect were considered from the teacher's point of view, and the "perspectives" required to build this environment in schools were listed. Perspectives

Table 2. Activity Model for Artistic Construction Activity

		Artistic Construction Activity	Activity Model
Essence		Continuity from life experience to artistic experience through the perception of qualities	
Methodological principle		Expression of the qualities of life experience through the construction of qualitative materials	
Structure	Process aspect	Fundamental point : "An experience" as artistic inquiry	
		Criteria Impulsion and resistance Creative problem-solving as inquiry Sharing of artworks as products	**Perspectives** Planning activity content that stimulates impulsion Setting up resistance to impulsion Checking the conditions for the establishment of expression Setting up a space to present artworks
	Psychological aspect	Fundamental point : Qualitative thinking through the psychosomatic interaction	
		Criteria Interaction of inner and outer (qualitative) materials Perception of the qualitative connections between "doing" and "undergoing" Circulation of the cycle of "observation–end-in-view–experiment" centered on images Multilayered thought structure of "body, image, and reflection"	**Perspectives** Actualization of inner and outer (qualitative) materials in life experience Setting up a space for observation via the perception methods of sensing and feeling Questioning toward the formation of an end-in-view Setting up a space for experiments
	Social aspect	Fundamental point : Communication of quality as the sharing of experience	
		Criteria Communication of quality in shared activities Formation of empathetic attitudes and community through the sharing of images	**Perspectives** Planning shared activities Setting up a space for the exchange of experiences in order to share images Encouraging multi-media communication Setting up a space for appreciation and critique in order to share artworks Valuing empathetic attitude and sense of coexistence

here refers to the point of view to be adopted by teachers attempting to conceive and put into practice artistic construction activity in order to build a learning environment. In practice, the various criteria function in organic connection, rather than in isolation. Therefore, notably, each perspective does not correspond one-to-one to each criterion.

Below is a discussion of the perspectives required to build an environment for artistic construction activity for each aspect. First, the fundamental points and criteria of each aspect are confirmed; next, the perspectives required to build an environment enabling their realization are explained.

Process aspect

1. Fundamental point and criteria

The process aspect concerns how artistic construction activity develops from beginning to end. The fundamental point of this aspect is "'an experience' as artistic inquiry." "An experience" refers to a unified process continuously developing from beginning to end with internal integration.

The criteria for realizing "'an experience' as artistic inquiry" include "impulsion and resistance," "creative problem-solving as inquiry," and "sharing of artworks as products."

To realize "'an experience' as artistic inquiry," first of all, impulsion must be stimulated and must encounter resistance. In encountering resistance, children sense disharmony with their environment. Inquiry thus begins, eventually concluding with the recovery of harmony and the creation of products. Thus, "an experience" is consummated.

This inquiry process develops for the children as the process of problem-solving. In artistic inquiry, which contains expression, the "problem" is the disharmony between the inner and outer materials of expression. This context involves not logical problem-solving, led by logic to converge on a single solution, but creative problem-solving, led by images to explore various solutions. The products are the artworks constructed by the children.

2. Perspectives for environment building

The perspectives required to build an environment that meets the above criteria can be listed as follows.

(1) Planning activity content that stimulates impulsion

First, impulsion must be stimulated. This is the problem of how to determine the subject and content of artistic construction activity. Here, the teacher focuses on the children's life experience and interests. The teachers get a casual sense of the children's daily lives and find materials the children are somewhat familiar with, or activities they are absorbed in. These are the impulsive acts the children will find themselves carrying out without thinking and the play that begins with an impulse. Examples include tapping on cups and bowls at the table, leaving footprints in a smooth stretch of sand, or drawing pictures with a finger on a fogged train window.

However, the simple fact that an activity is impulsive does not necessarily render it sufficient. The teacher must consider whether these impulsive acts have the potential to develop into culture and art. For example, let us consider the impulsive act of tapping on nearby objects. Because tapping on various objects creates a range of sounds with unique timbres, the teacher reasons that the action of tapping can be developed into a percussion ensemble making use of timbres. The teacher thus creates the classroom environment by using string to hang up clay planters, stainless steel bowls, and so on. Then, the teacher plans the activity content. It begins when the children impulsively strike the hanging objects, after which they combine the sounds thus discovered and create music in groups, making the most of the timbres they found.

Because artistic construction activity begins with impulsion, teachers are called on first to locate the children's life experiences and interests, to consider the prospects for developing these into culture and art, and to plan the subject and content of the activity based thereon.

94

(2) Setting up resistance to impulsion

When impulsion has been stimulated, the teacher's next duty is to set up resistance to it. If left to impulsive activity as is, the children will not manage to express themselves. Therefore, the teacher sets up a form of resistance for them. For example, recording and replaying the performances given by the children, absorbed in the activity through impulsion, can serve as resistance. Replaying the recording for the children causes them to become aware of the results of their actions. The replayed performances are the results of the children's own actions, so they are extremely personal. The children will be eager to listen. Now, if they sense disharmony ("something weird"), the situation becomes "uncertain," the desire to do things differently emerges, and the interaction with materials for problem-solving begins.

Cultural materials (those constructing culture) can also serve as resistance. Cultural materials are the accumulated products created as our predecessors followed the path of inquiry from impulsion. For example, resistance can be created when the teacher sees children striking objects at random to make sounds and suggests that they use the basic ostinato technique of constructing sounds. The children begin to think about what patterns of sounds to make. However, the suggestion of cultural materials must be positioned as an extension of the children's impulsive activity. It is important to find a method that will work as resistance within the children's impulsive activity currently in progress, rather than bringing in resistance from outside.

(3) Checking the conditions for the establishment of expression

Through their encounter with resistance, the children reflect on their impulsive activity and enter the indirect channel to expression. At this point, the teacher must check whether their activities will lead to expression based on the conditions for expression to be established. These conditions include "expressive media," "joining of old and new experiences," and "modes of response of the doer."

The checking process includes the following. Regarding "expressive media," are the materials being used as a means to the end of expressing something? Regarding the "joining of old and new experiences," are "doing" and "undergoing" connected via images? Regarding the "modes of response of the doer," is the activity in progress suited to the children's current conditions and abilities?

The teacher is called on to check on the children's activities in progress based on these conditions in order to enable their interaction with sound materials to become expressive activity.

(4) Setting up a space to present artworks

Artworks are created as the products of inquiry. They take shape through the interaction of inner and outer materials, which is consummated when inner and outer materials are unified, that is, when a "certain situation" has been recovered. First, the teacher confirms whether the activity has reached a "certain situation" in which the children are satisfied.

Next, rather than assessing the quality of the artworks alone, distinct from the process, the teacher grasps the artworks as continuous with the process the children have worked through. For instance, one option would be, when having the children perform their artwork (performance), to ask them to present the points they put effort into, their intentions, images, and so on along with the performance.

In artistic inquiry, the artworks created as products exist not as general and instrumental, but as individual and self-contained. It is important for the teacher be conscious of the position of grasping the artworks as expressions of the children's individuality, and to create a space for appreciation and critique of the artworks, sharing them within the social microcosm of the class.

Psychological aspect

1. Fundamental point and criteria

The psychological aspect of artistic construction activity relates to how children interact with materials. The fundamental point of this aspect is "qualitative thinking through psychosomatic interaction." The criteria for realizing this point include "interaction of inner and outer (qualitative) materials," "perception of the qualitative connections between 'doing' and 'undergoing'," "circulation of the cycle of 'observation–end-in-view–experiment' centered on images," and "multilayered thought structure of 'body, image, and reflection'."

2. Perspectives for environment building

The perspectives required to build an environment that meets the above criteria can be listed as follows.

(1) Actualization of inner and outer (qualitative) materials in life experience

Without materials, there can be no expression. First, children must be provided with materials, which may serve as inner or outer materials. "Provided" here does not mean that the teacher bestows the materials from the outside; rather, they only manifest those already latent in the children. The teacher promotes the children's awareness of the thoughts and feelings cultivated and accumulated in their experiences of daily life and school, enabling them to use these as inner materials. The same applies with outer materials, as familiar materials from experiences of daily life and school are put to use. The sounds, musical composition elements, methods, and techniques that act as outer materials derive their original models from life experience. Examples of this include repetition, change, contrast, question-and-answer, and so on. When composing sounds, children naturally adopt the methods and forms they have experienced in daily life, without needing to be taught.

In short, providing children with materials in artistic construction activity means that the teacher finds the materials within the children's life experience and makes the children aware of them. The teacher's role is to find meaning and value in the sounds, musical composition elements, techniques, and forms latent within life experience that the children recall as well as to promote awareness of their forms so as to lead to culture and art.

(2) Setting up a space for observation via the perception methods of sensing and feeling

To realize "circulation through the cycle of 'observation–end-in-view–experiment' centered on images," observation is important. The children observe the "facts," that is the products, as the results undergone through doing.

The thinking that occurs during interactions between the inner and outer materials of expression is qualitative reflective thinking based on the interaction of mind and body. Here, the connections between "doing" and "undergoing" is qualitative. Qualitative relationships are perceived through the methods of sensing and feeling. "Sensing" in this case means perceiving the elements or structure of the target through the physical senses, and "feeling" means intuiting the qualities of the target. The simultaneous connection of these two operations enables the perception of the qualitative connections between "doing" and "undergoing."

However, children tend to be biased toward production of works, and they have trouble taking a step back to observe their products objectively. Therefore, when the children have made a certain amount of progress in production, the teacher is called on to create an intentional space for observation. One way to do this is to record and play back the children's performances for objective observation. This means creating a space where the children can observe the facts of what they have done and what the results were. Production (doing) of art is educed through perception (undergoing), and takes on unity.

(3) Questioning toward the formation of an end-in-view

When a space for observation has been created, the next step is to have the children themselves connect what they have done and its results. In qualitative thinking, "doing" and "undergoing" are connected via the mediation of images. Here, the teacher's role is to question what the children have observed and their images. The perception of qualities is difficult to express verbally. Therefore, it is difficult for the children to become aware of what they have observed and their images on their own. Often, they may feel something and yet not realize they have done so. Furthermore, for the children themselves, putting what they feel into words is unnecessary. Unless questioned by others, the children will not become aware of their images nor put them into words. Images act as a guiding light for interaction, so that if the children remain unaware of their images, their manipu-

98

lation of outer materials will remain capricious or mechanical.

When questioned, the children *try* to put their images into words. "Trying" enables them to become aware of the qualitative relationship between "doing" and "undergoing." Through awareness of this relationship, they get a glimpse of their next step, what they want to do next. This next step is the "end-in-view."

The teacher leads the children to sense and feel qualitative relationships, questions them on what they have sensed and felt, and promotes awareness by having the children put this in their own words, enabling the formation of an end-in-view: "Let's try this next." Thus, the cycle of "observation – end-in-view – experiment" centered on images is set in motion.

(4) Setting up a space for experiments

The children form an end-in-view based on what they have observed (sensed, felt). This end-in-view must be tested via experiments. If the concepts and hypotheses of the end-in-view are not put into practice, inquiry will be halted. By experimenting with the end-in-view, the activity gains direction.

Therefore, after observation, the teacher must set up a space for experiments in order to circulate the cycle of "observation–end-in-view–experiment." When the children produce an end-in-view, the teacher encourages them to try it out, creating actual sounds.

However, the end-in-view as a hypothesis is not going to take form instantly. In artistic construction activity, "trial-and-error experiments" testing various ideas that come to mind are essential as the groundwork to form an end-in-view. Thus, in artistic construction activity, experiments include "trial-and-error experiments" and "end-in-view experiments." The latter are established based on the former, circulating the "observation–end-in-view– experiment" cycle.

Trial-and-error experiments. Experiments in artistic inquiry differ from those in scientific inquiry, which verify the logical relationships between methods and results. In artistic inquiry, rather than focusing exclusively on problem-solving, significance is placed on meandering and playing. The space for experiments as a form of play, trying various things out, serves as the fount of creativity. Therefore, it is important that rather than trying to lead the children straight to solving the problem, the teacher provides time and space for them to play and experiment freely with outer materials, that is, to conduct trial-and-error experiments.

End-in-view experiments. The other form of experimentation is end-in-view experiments. The role of the teacher includes encouraging children to experiment, inviting them to try out their ideas. The end-in-view is a hypothesis predicting that a certain action will produce a certain result based on observation. In end-in-view experiments, the relationship between "doing" and "undergoing" becomes extremely personal and more strongly perceived, seeing how the facts change depending on the actions taken. Therefore, children come to *pay close attention* to the results of the experiment, making it easier for them to grasp the meaning. The meaning provides guidance for the next action (doing).

When experimenting with the end-in-view, music as an external fact is "recreated." When the recreated music is observed, it acquires meaning, thus recreating the end-in-view as well. End-in-view experiments thus further and guide the interaction between inner and outer materials. However, school group activities usually have a bias toward discussion, and the children are slow to try out the sounds in practice. The teacher is called on to encourage the children to take action on the plans they have come up with as a group. As this process is repeated, it should lead to the cultivation of an experimental attitude in the children.

Social aspect

1. Fundamental point and criteria

The social aspect of artistic construction activity addresses how children relate to others. The fundamental point of this aspect is "communication of quality as the sharing of experience." Artistic construction activity is performed in relation to others, not by individuals in isolation. Here, communication is important. Communication in artistic construction activity is mainly communication of qualities, exchanging experiences of qualities.

The criterion for realizing this point is "communication of quality in shared activities." Children perform artistic construction activity as a shared activity in order to share experiences. The experiences to be shared in the activity are those of qualities; this exchange is conducted as the communication of quality in order to share images.

Images and qualities cannot be conveyed through verbal concepts. The communication of quality thus requires the will and attitude to guess at the qualities sensed by the other person, that is, the empathetic attitude of putting oneself the other's shoes. This empathetic attitude leads to the formation of a community. This relates to "formation of empathetic attitudes and community through the sharing of images."

2. Perspectives for environment building

The perspectives required to build an environment that realizes the above criteria can be listed as follows.

(1) Planning shared activities

In artistic construction activity, the environment is designed to bring individuals into contact with one another, facilitating communication. To this end, the teacher plans a "shared activity" in which the children have a common end and construct a "shared object." The conditions for the shared object are that the inner and outer materials, which are its components, derive from the children's life experience, and there are prospects for the construction of a unified whole of some kind using these materials.

While shared activity takes the form of creating a single artwork as a group, expressive activity performed alone as individuals is also possible. However, there must be a plan for the individual artwork to become part of the shared activity as well, resulting in a unified artwork of some kind when the individual artworks are connected and integrated.

(2) Setting up a space for the exchange of experiences in order to share images

Shared activity requires a space for the exchange of individual experiences. First,

the teacher creates a space for children to work face-to-face, so that they can observe one another's activities. Communication here is mainly the communication of
qualities, focused on topics related to images. However, because images are difficult to put into words, the communication is rarely smooth.

At this point, the teacher must stop the children's group activities, switch to a
full-class format, and create an intentional space for the exchange of experiences.
This space is considered to allow reflection when a problem of some kind arises,
something is expressed with a new concept, or the situation changes. The topics
discussed include the connections between the done and the undergone, observations, and experiments on the end-in-view. Intermediate presentations on
performance are positioned here as well. The teacher is called on to organize the
space so that the full-class format will provide opportunities for children to exchange experiences and expand their mutual experience through give-and-take,
playing the role of the facilitator who brings the children in contact with each other.

This space for the exchange of experiences is necessary in order to keep the children constantly aware of the shared object. The works created as the shared object
of artistic construction activity are qualitative. In the case of music in particular,
the sounds produced are ephemeral. It is important for the teacher to manage a
space for the exchange of experiences, bearing in mind the need to regularly give
voice to the target music.

(3) Encouraging multi-media communication

In order to share images in this space for the exchange of experiences, communication via multiple media (gestures, sounds, onomatopoeia, pictures, etc.) is required.
It is important for the teacher to use this space to question the children ("how would
you express this with movements?" "can you make sounds imitating it?" "what color would
it be if it was a color?") and to encourage them to use various media to express their
images. Therefore, during the process of artistic construction activity, the teacher
must make it a point to encourage the children to share their images at any time,
by creating a space for multi-media communication.

At the same time, language is also a powerful medium for communication within this space. Prompting the children to use metaphors in verbal communication makes it easier for them to convey to others the qualities they perceive and images. However, the teacher is called on to ensure that verbal communication acts to support and complement multi-media communication, rather than standing alone.

(4) Setting up a space for appreciation and critique in order to share artworks

The products of artistic construction activity are "artworks." Art can be defined as the communication of qualities between a producer and a perceiver with the artwork as the medium. Therefore, the children must share their artworks with others in order to find them satisfactory as products. The final stage thus calls for a space for mutual appreciation and critique of the finished artworks. Critique enables the producer to gain an external viewpoint and to apply new meanings to their artwork. The teacher must take steps to make the artworks heard as needed, so that the communication between listener and producer is not reduced to language alone.

(5) Valuing empathetic attitude and sense of coexistence

Artistic construction activity is the shared process of constructing together a shared object with a common end. In shared activity, becoming involved in the expressions of others leads to interest in what the others are doing. Thus, emotional communication is facilitated (encouraging someone who is struggling, praising them when they succeed).

Artistic construction activity is centered on the communication of qualities. Because it is impossible to discuss qualities through verbal concepts, the communication of qualities relies on will, attitude, and emotion to guess at and imagine from the shared object how the other person has expressed the qualities they sensed in sound, physical movement, color, or form; that is, what qualities they sensed and what images went through their mind. In short, without an empathetic attitude, the communication of qualities between children cannot take place. The empathetic attitude also creates a sense of community among the group. The teacher must value this kind of emotional communication to be found within artistic construction activity. This stance will indirectly lead to the cultivation of an empathetic attitude.

Example of activity model in practice

Activity model for artistic construction activity was discussed in the previous part. This part presents an example of how activity models is realized in practice.

Obviously, in practice, the process, psychological, and social aspects become an integrated whole. To show how each of the perspectives for environment building presented with the activity models is realized in practice, a practice case is approached from the process, psychological, and social aspects.

The case chosen here is a practice conducted by the author at H Elementary School in Kanoashi County, Shimane Prefecture, Japan, in 1978. In this activity, children brought from their homes objects that made sounds they liked, formed groups, and created music. In a combined fifth-and-sixth-grade class, a group of two fifth-graders and one sixth-grader, all boys, made "Steam Train" music (See Writing Score1: Steam Train).

The teacher took the position that artworks as expression were created not through external instruction on techniques but in connection with the students' inner worlds, aiming at the double change, inner and outer, which is at the core of artistic construction activity. The main methods used were (1) having the children choose themes for their artworks from their own life experience, (2) providing them with sufficient time and space to interact with sound, and (3) creating a space for reflection by having children listen to recordings of their own performances as needed. Because the intention of this research was to explore the children's thinking, the instructions provided by the teacher to the children were minimal.

Process aspect

1. Planning activity content that stimulates impulsion

As sound-making objects, the children brought glasses, lunch plates, and so on from home. The teacher had each child introduce their tools' sounds to the class, and then divided them into groups to make music. At first, the children seemed to find the act of striking the tools interesting in itself, doing so as they pleased and becoming absorbed in the process and the sounds that resulted. When they formed groups and struck their tools together, each group gradually developed its own beat, and individuals created subdivided-rhythms and improvised along with it.

The impulsive behavior of striking objects to create a sound, which is seen from infancy, serves as the activity content stimulating impulsion. The emergence of free improvisation therein suggests that impulsion has found an object, becoming interest in the act of creating a rhythm by striking sound-making objects. Here the prospect that this activity will develop into a percussion ensemble can be discerned.

2. Setting up resistance to impulsion

At this point, the teacher recorded the improvised performances and played them back. The children complained that "it's all over the place" or "the ending is too weak," and tried to find solutions, saying "what will we do?" Reflecting on the situation, they came up with the concept of "adding dynamics in waves." They then tried it out.

Thus, the teacher set up a space for "resistance" by having the children listen to the recordings. The children encountered resistance and found themselves in an "uncertain situation," sensing a problem. From there inquiry began. As the desire to create a satisfying performance arose, the children went through reflection and entered creative problem-solving as inquiry.

3. Checking the conditions for the establishment of expression

In the process of inquiry, the teacher checked whether the children's actions were expressive. The children listened to a recording of their own performance after experimenting with "adding dynamics in waves," and the teacher asked them what it felt like. They answered with images like "the feeling of a steam train running."

Here, the teacher's intent in asking the children "what does it feel like?" was to bring together old and new experience (the joining of old and new experiences). When asked about their images, the children recalled older experiences, imagining their music as a steam train running. They joined their past experience of steam trains to the present experience of music-making, doing their best to create sounds like a steam train. The teacher checked whether the outer material, the glass sound, was acting as an expressive medium for the image (expressive media), whether the children could strike the glasses so as to give the sense of a steam train's rhythm, and whether their imagination was expanding to encompass, for instance, the steam train sounding its whistle as it goes through a tunnel (modes of response of the doer). The teacher questioned the children so that their actions would take on the conditions for the establishment of expression.

4. Setting up a space to present artworks

Finally, the teacher set up a space for the artwork (performance) in the class. The "Steam Train" group's performance represented a train leaving the station, picking up speed, going past signals, going through a tunnel, sounding its whistle, going across a railway bridge, and slowing down to arrive at the next station. The children became absorbed in their performance, as if they themselves had become the train, or as if they were aboard the train and excitedly watching the view. This was the "artwork as a product." This performance used musical composition elements, forms, techniques, and methods such as rhythm, timbre, tempo, dynamics, form, and so on; the initial actions, in which each child struck their cup as they liked, had been integrated into a unified artwork with diverse expressions of the steam train's passage. This served as a "certain situation," where the children were satisfied and the inquiry was consummated.

Psychological aspect

1. Actualization of inner and outer (qualitative) materials in life experience

The teacher assigned the students to bring in an object that made a sound they liked. This assignment enabled the students to become newly aware of familiar sounds in their life, such as hitting a glass with a spoon. It provided the children with outer materials, and at the same time with inner materials. The act of choosing a favorite sound was performed through the interaction between inner materials (the image of the timbre of the glass) and outer materials (the sound of the glass).

In class, both inner and outer materials were recreated through their interaction. The children drew sound from their sound-making objects (glasses, etc.) as outer materials, while having images of "the feeling of a steam train running" as inner materials. The phenomenon of the steam train includes "changes of tempo." Here, the musical composition element of "tempo" was used as an outer material. When the tempo of the performance changed, the images of entering the tunnel, crossing the bridge, and so on emerged one after another, with the timbre and rhythm changing along with the images. The images appearing here as inner materials are those drawn from life experience. The tempo, dynamics, timbre, and rhythm, as outer materials, are likewise the elements constructing life experience.

In artistic construction activity, inner and outer materials come to light in this way from life experience. However, this calls for the teacher to question the children about their life experience and images. Questioning provides an opportunity for the materials to come to light.

2. Setting up a space for observation via the perception methods of sensing and feeling

The teacher recorded the children's performances and played them back at key moments. This constituted setting up a space for the children to observe how what they did affected their performance, that is, a space for reflection. The children were thus enabled to perceive the connections between "doing" and "undergoing."

Naturally, there is no need to record every single moment. As the activity neared its end, the children started to focus on their performances while performing, and as soon as they finished, to express their opinions such as "I still think there's something weird about the end." However, even once children reach the point of being able to perceive their own performances, the use of the recordings is still significant. By adopting the stance of perceivers and listening to themselves perform, they become capable of observation of the whole, rather than only a part of the music. Deliberately setting up a space for them to observe objectively what they have done is essential in enabling the children themselves to find the way to their next action.

3. Questioning toward the formation of an end-in-view

The children always acquired ideas of some kind from listening to the recordings. The teacher questioned them to have them put their ideas into words. The children did so, along the lines of "it's all over the place and it isn't coming together." Putting the problem into words enabled them to become aware of it as a problem. In order to resolve the problem, they had the idea of "adding dynamics in waves." This concept was both a "means" of problem-solving and an "end" for the next action, serving as a glimpse of the desired "result." In short, it was an "end-in-view." By putting their ideas into words, the children can further their thinking. This requires a situation in which they are questioned by another person about what is going through their minds.

4. Setting up a space for experiments

The children's ideas were tested in experiments. These included trial-and-error experiments and end-in-view experiments.

(1) Trial-and-error experiments

Let us consider the moment when the children making the steam train music decided to add a bridge-crossing part. They remembered that the timbre of the train changes when it crosses a bridge. Trying to find the timbre of the bridge-crossing sounds, they struck various items in the classroom. Among them, they found materials that suited them. While striking these items, they remembered that the rhythm of the steam train changes when it crosses the bridge, tried out various rhythms, and found the one they liked.

This can be considered a *trial-and-error* experiment. However, the children's actions were not limited to trial-and-error. They were searching for the timbres and rhythms suited to the images in their minds. Their method was to search for the outer materials of timbre and rhythm while trying out various actions. This was their trial-and-error experiment. Based on this experiment, the end-in-view came into sight.

(2) End-in-view experiments

While children sometimes move spontaneously to experimenting with an end-in-view, this rarely happens when they are not familiar with experiments. At this point, it is important for the teacher to encourage them to experiment, to try things out.

When the children make "observations" that their own performance lacked unity and acquired the "end-in-view" of adding dynamics in waves, the teacher encouraged them to "experiment" and try things out. Thus encouraged, the children performed with the end-in-view of adding dynamics. In short, they experimented. Then, the teacher had them listen to their own recordings and questioned them about what it felt like. The children answered with images like "the feeling of a steam train running." Other members of the group nodded in agreement, showing that the image was shared among the group. The children were able to give the meaningless clatter of a spoon on a glass the meaning of "the sound of a steam train running."

Here we find the cycle of "observation–end-in-view–experiment" centered on images, as well as the perception of the qualitative relationship between "doing" and "undergoing." "Doing" here is changing the musical compositional element of dynamics, and "undergoing" is listening to the performance with the changed dynamics and finding the image of "the feeling of a steam train running" there. The music with the changed dynamics is sensed, and the qualities it creates are felt through images; in short, the perception of qualities through sensing and feeling takes place.

The background of this image formation is the qualitative perception of past life experience (the rhythmic strength of the vibrations when riding a train, etc.). Imagination is what brings to mind the past experience of riding a steam train and connects it to the present experience of making music. The formed image gives qualitative meaning to the resonance created from the sounds of striking glasses and lunch plates in the present, as "music that feels like the train did." In the cycle of "observation–end-in-view–experiment," the artwork is given meaning through the formation of images. In order to have children form the images that lead interactions, this cycle must be circulated; to that end, it is important that the teacher consciously encourages the children to experiment with an end-in-view.

Social aspect

1. Planning shared activities

The teacher planned an activity in which the children would bring in sound-making objects (glasses, lunch plates, etc.) and strike them together in groups. At first, the children were absorbed in the act of striking the tools themselves, but after doing so in groups a few times, a beat naturally emerged. When they began to feel the beat, each group member inserted their own micro-rhythms or improvisations into the overall rhythm.

In terms of the social aspect, given that each group member brought in their own possessions (sound-making objects) for the activity, and a certain beat was shared throughout the group, this performance can be considered the group's "shared object." Shared activity was established when the group of three boys set the common end of making music together. That is, the end to be shared did not exist from the start. The common end was set through actions, and the activity became a shared one through the common end. Thereafter, as the image became segmented, each group member's sound had its own role. For instance, C child played the sound of crossing the bridge, and A child the sound of the train whistle. As the three children shared a common end, each taking up their own role and coordinating with the others, the activity moved toward creating a single piece of music.

2. Setting up a space for the exchange of experiences in order to share images

As artistic construction activity is shared activity, the group members naturally talk with one another during the process. This is a good opportunity for the exchange of experiences. However, the teacher must also set up a space consciously intended for the exchange of experiences. That is, because experience in artistic construction activity is qualitative, the group members must share their images with one another. Expressing images through words is basically impossible. However, if the images are not expressed externally in some form, the exchange of related experiences will not take place, and the images will be unlikely be broadened or deepened. Here, the teacher is called on to question the children about their images.

When the group was working on and performing its train music, the teacher asked about images: "What kind of steam train?" "A local." "Not such a nice train." "A kind of old battered train," the children answered. Questioning them about their images brought to their attention what kind of train they had in mind. As the members answered, each in their own phrasing, the vague original image of "a steam train" became segmented ("an old battered local steam train") and shared. From this segmented image, the group members proposed more and more concepts: a level crossing, an alarm, entering a tunnel, crossing a railway bridge, and so on.

By putting their images into words this way, they were able to deepen and expand both their own and others' images. Through intentionally creating a space for the exchange of experiences, both in small groups and in the full-class format, the activity was further developed.

3. Encouraging multi-media communication

For perspective2, "the exchange of experiences in order to share images," to be successful, multi-media communication is effective. When children try spontaneously to convey their images to others, they gesture, sketch pictures, or make sounds as they speak. These actions are not carried out in a self-aware manner. The children are naturally using qualitative media such as physical movement, pictures, or sound in search of other expressive media, to express what words cannot.

The use of these multiple media, however, may not always arise spontaneously in the children. They often struggle to find a way to convey their own thoughts and images. In this case, the teacher can effectively encourage them to use multiple media: "Why not draw a picture?" or "Show us with movements." Encouraging verbal communication simultaneously with multi-media communication, with the latter supported and complemented by words, enables qualitative thinking in children.

4. Setting up a space for appreciation and critique in order to share artworks

Finally, a concert was held for the class to appreciate and critique each group's artwork. The steam train group gave the following performance. The train set off from the station, putting on speed. It passed by signals and through a tunnel, sounded its whistle, and crossed a railway bridge. Finally, it slowed down and arrived at the next station, where the performance ended.

The children were absorbed in their performance, as if truly becoming the train as it ran along the tracks. The author, in the same situation, likewise observed the performance and became absorbed in the music, envisioning the train puffing energetically faster and faster ahead and the varied scenery of its travel. The children in the other groups, the perceivers, also commented that "it was like being on a train. I felt like I was riding through the mountains," adding their own color to the images. The image of "riding through the mountains" was a new one, which had not arisen in conversation within the performing group. The experience of others had given their performance this new meaning. This can be considered the "sharing of the artwork."

5. Valuing empathetic attitude and sense of coexistence

C child, one of the boys in the "Steam Train" group, happened to have found a test tube in the science room. Engaged with the steam train music-making, he wondered if this tube, normally used in science class, would make a sound like a train whistle. He picked it up and puffed experimentally. His fellow group members saw this and encouraged him: "Nice one, C!" "Keep practicing!" As the whistling sound emerged and was met with applause, the encouragement continued: "You go, C! Keep practicing!" The applause and encouragement here indicated the appearance of empathy, putting oneself in another's shoes.

C child had acquired the end-in-view of using the test tube he found by chance to represent the train whistle. However, when he experimented with it, the technically difficult whistling sound was hard to obtain. C practiced over and over, indicating his attitude of interest and at the same time of effort. When he managed an approximation of the sound, his fellow group members rejoiced and applauded, engaged with his achievement, encouraging him with an empathetic attitude.

The social aspect of artistic construction activity cultivates this kind of empathetic attitude, as well as a sense of coexistence, of living with others. While the teacher cannot intentionally create interpersonal relations like these, paying attention to the value of this kind of emotional aspect, which is so notable in artistic construction activity, may ultimately lead to the cultivation of empathetic attitudes and a sense of coexistence.

Overview of the children in practice

Above is an explanation of the condition of the children taking part in a practice case, seen from the process, psychological, and social aspects. However, in actual practice, these three aspects are integrated and unified. In conclusion, let us go over the condition of the children in the practice of this activity, where integration of these three aspects has taken place, when viewed from the outside. This is what they look like.

While the children are engaging in impulsive sound play, they acquire the objective of expressive something and consider how best to do it. When they think, they make actual sounds, listen to the result, obtain an image, and with that image as a guide, conceive and attempt the next operation. Over the process of this activity, they communicate via words and movements with their friends, exchanging opinions, ideas, images, and arising concerns on the target music. Finally, they create a unified artwork and present it to the class.

114

Writhing Scorel : Steam Train

⟨terminal station⟩

Chapter

Typical Artistic Construction Activities

This chapter introduces four types of typical artistic construction activities that use sound as their material: music-making, instrument-making, song-writing, and graphic score-making[1]. The core materials in the interaction of inner and outer materials differ among these four types of activities. The different core materials create different characteristics for each activity. These characteristics are illustrated through examples of practice, led by the author.

In terms of the format, first, an overview of the activity is provided. Next, the basic stance taken to the activity and its characteristics are described.

Music-making

Overview: The activity of music-making is launched from images in life experience. In this activity, students choose and combine sounds freely to express striking images from their own life experience, such as lighting sparklers on a summer evening or watching cicadas emerge. When they try to make sounds in order to express their images, the relevant life experience is brought to mind. This creates segmentation of the previously vague images. In music-making, this interaction of sounds with images from life experience is especially clear.

The sounds that serve as materials are sought not only from instruments but also widely throughout the environment of daily life, including cups, bamboo leaves, and so on. The methods for constructing sounds are found within the children's own life experience to date. These methods are often marked by an originality reminiscent of the methods of contemporary music.

Finally, the images from life experience are constructed to form a unified artwork, creating expressions possessed of reality for the children. In the sense that life experience connects directly to expression, this can be said to be the prototype of artistic construction activity.

Stances

"Music-making" is different from "composition," i.e., making music by writing notes on staff paper. The former refers to an activity in which children improvise sounds to construct their artwork, freely exploring their own ideas without the mediation of musical notes or staff notation and without absolute conformity to any specific form of music theory.

Notable here, however, is that there are two stances regarding music-making. The first considers it a way to learn musical techniques and language, while the second regards it as a form of artistic construction activity, as proposed in this book.

The former values the use of techniques and language consistent with the artworks of composers in the artworks created by children, which are to have a specific musical form, so that the activity does not simply constitute sound play. Its roots are in contemporary music, and its aim, as a learning activity, is the mastery of the techniques and language of contemporary music in order to realize diverse sound materials and musical formats in the finished artworks. The artworks are evaluated according to their completion in terms of musical language and format, with a focus on musical unity.

The latter, music-making as artistic construction activity, is rooted not in contemporary music but in children's inherent desire for expression. Its focus is not, like the former, on how skillfully sounds can be combined, but on how the child's inner world, created through experience of the outer world, can be expressed through sound.

Common to both stances is the creation of musical artworks through repeating the experimental use of improvisation with sounds, rather than relying on staff notation, while addressing the various materials of sound. However, while the former focuses on the unity of the piece distinct from the inner world of the children's thoughts and images, the latter, music-making in artistic construction activity, focuses on this inner world. Naturally, the latter also pursues the unity of the artwork in order to satisfy the children themselves and to share the artworks with others. However, that unity is not imposed externally through the teacher's guidance, but created through the children's own thinking and inquiry as they bear images in mind.

While the children's artworks as products of artistic construction activity end up bearing many similarities to contemporary music in musical technique and language, in this context they are considered, if anything, forms and modes of human life experience. In fact, as the children bring their own life experience to mind, they reflect in the compositional principles of their artworks the modes and forms of this experience, such as "repetition and change" or "appearance and disappearance." At the same time, the images and feelings of life experience are integrated within the form of the artwork. In this way, the fundamental human practice of expression is enacted with a sense of reality for the children, based on life experience: this is the value of music-making as artistic construction activity.

Characteristics

1. The joining of life experiences and expression through interest

Themes are considered important in music-making. Children choose a theme and use it as a starting point. While they may also start from a sound, they are still beginning with a theme, set based on the images that arise from the sound. The theme is not simply a random inspiration; it is important that it is selected from experiences in life, that is, interaction with the outside world. The selection of the theme determines whether the music-making can go forward based on life experience.

The importance of this theme setting is due to the influence of individual sensations and interests in selecting among life experiences. This is where the outer world of life experience and the inner world of the children's sensibilities and interests come into contact. The scope of selection may include the natural world (snow, rain, showers, wind), the ecology of the flora and fauna therein, the work of the people living there, festivals, events such as Christmas, fireworks, and so on.

One practice case used "Blacksmith" as the theme for music-making. Blacksmithing is a form of work. The blacksmith's work is to "forge iron, striking off sparks," with an internal movement in which all the elements are integrated toward the purpose. This movement can be possessed of what Dewey called aesthetic quality. This may be why music and paintings with blacksmiths as their theme have been common for many years in both Japan and the West. In 1970s Japan, when this practice took place, smiths forging iron were still an everyday sight. The children, fascinated by the motion, sound, and sparks as the iron was forged, wanted to express what they perceived. Their images included both the overall perception of the blacksmith and also the individual images of "sparks flying," "the sound of the iron being heated and struck with a hammer during forging," and so on. The images are elicited by actions. When pretending to be a blacksmith and making the right sounds, the images of the smithy such as sparks flying are elicited (See Writing Score 2: Blacksmith[2]).

The selection of a theme from life experience leads an awareness of the individual's inner world, integrating interests, images, and feelings. This provokes the desire for expression, leading to the joining of the outer world with the world of expression.

2. The logic of the outer world that creates the expressive form

In order to give shape to the inner world through expression, the sound materials must be combined and take form. Here, the children find within their life experience the methods and formats that give shape to the sound materials. At this point, the children rely on the logic of the outer world for hints. Phenomena in the outer world are possessed of forms of some kind.

The children who chose "Sparklers" as their theme began with the soft ring of wind chimes and subsequently layered percussive rhythm patterns. At the high point, they used the sound of crumpled plastic bags to express the brilliant effect. After that, the sounds dropped out one by one. Finally the wind chimes sounded once again, soft amid the quiet, and the piece ended. Here, the "appearance and disappearance" format of the sparklers was adopted for the music. Outer world phenomena follow the logic of "if X, then Y," and this logic reveals their forms. Among these is the form of "appearance and disappearance." The children drew on the forms of phenomena they had experienced in daily life, using them for expression in music. Thus, the sound materials were ordered, arranged, and constructed into a music artwork. In short, the logic of phenomena is converted into the logic of expression.

3. The qualities of the outer world that create expressive matter

The phenomena of the outer world not only hint at form, but at the same time create the children's inner images, that is, the expressive matter of the music.

The third-graders who chose "Picking Horsetails" as their theme expressed the life cycle of the horsetail plant, from emerging from the dirt to wilting and spreading spores. Like "Sparklers" above, this piece expressed the form of "appearance and disappearance." However, rather than simply following the facts of horsetail growth objectively, the piece anthropomorphized the horsetail as a family, expressing the images created by the children's imagination. First, the horsetail pops up here and there from the ground; as the family members appear one after the next, they all begin to dance. There, a drum, bell, and bamboo whisk join the music. The children must have imagined the horsetails as a family and felt a sense of excitement when seeing them growing in a group, as if they were all enjoying a dance together. This image was probably derived from the qualities experienced when picking horsetails. In order to figure out how to express these images in sound, the children used bouncy, happy-sounding rhythm patterns, experimented with popping sounds on their instruments, and gently tore tissue paper for the wilting scene. These ideas and techniques, drawn from their own images, create the expressive qualities that constitute the music. That is, the images possessed of the qualities of the phenomena create the matter of the expression.

Song-writing

Overview: Song-writing begins with the children's own spoken language. This activity expresses their own inner worlds through turning their spoken language into songs. Conditions include that the children are speaking in their first language, which they use in daily life, and that the words are their own, emerging from within, rather than those of others. Spoken language involves a prosodic aspect (the pitch, rhythm, and dynamics of the voice) as well as a semantic aspect that leads to images and feelings. The two are interrelated. When inner feelings grow intense, word inflection is emphasized; vowel sounds may be extended, or the rhythm of speech may bounce. Through these interactions, spoken language becomes song. This requires someone to hear the speech or song as a prerequisite. We speak to a listener. The listener may even be another part of ourselves.

By putting their own experience into words and making the words into a song, the children perceive and objectivize the feelings and images they have experienced in daily life. The tangled feelings of adolescence are given shape in the form of a song; at the same time, through the interaction with words as materials and the adjustment of syllable pitch, rhythm, and dynamics, they construct an objective artwork.

Stances

Of the two stances on song-writing, one views it as melodic creation intended to create melodies and musical lines, while the other considers it artistic construction activity.

In the former view, melodic creation may include, for example, continuing on from the beginning of a melody written on staff paper, or using a specific scale to improvise a melody on a recorder. The goal is to learn musical compositional elements and music theory through creating melodies. This kind of activity has long been a part of Japanese textbooks for music classes. The focus is on the external creation of a melody based on music theory, with no view taken on the children's interiority.

The latter, song-writing as artistic construction activity, is fundamentally different from the former in that the song begins with spoken language, not with notes or scales. This is derived from the stance taken by artistic construction activity, which returns to the primordial origins of human music. In song-writing, the act of singing is considered continuous with speaking words, chanting, and storytelling.

With regard to the origins of music among humans, the cognitive archaeologist Steven Mithen argues that in prehistory, music and language were one and the same (Mithen, 2006). According to this theory, both music and language used the vocal organs as tools for auditory communication. This communication is thought to have been a holistic format in which feelings and thoughts were integrated, including facial expressions and gestures as well as speech not yet segmented into words. This speech was then divided into the two products of music and language. Because singing is an expression that combines music and language, it is an action powerfully invoking the function of holistic communication integrating the entire human inner world of feelings and thoughts.

Songs tell stories in words, and these stories express various emotions in daily life. Various qualities are experienced in life. The experience of qualities is always accompanied by emotion. The sound of speech is made into music with emphasis on its rhythm and inflection, enabling the expression of the emotions associated with the situation. The expression of emotion is an important element of spoken language. Therefore, in song-writing where spoken words become songs, the words that become the lyrics are also important in terms of the children's self-expression. This approach does not provide existing texts written by someone else from the outside and have the children fit melodies to them. The focus is on the process of narrating the words emerging from the inner self as a melody.

Characteristics

1. The integration of words, voice, and physical movement

The desire to sing, which is essential for a song to emerge, requires cultivation in the right environment. This environment is daily life. In life experience, words, voice, and physical movement are integrated. When one is moved by something in this environment, the desire to convey this feeling to other people arises, and words emerge and become a song.

Songs in daily life often emerge amid the mutual interplay of words, voice, and physical movement. Voice is emitted in integration with physical movement, such as nursery rhymes during play, traditional songs performed at festivals, hawkers' calls, fishermen and farmers' work calls, and so on. Song-writing based on everyday life focuses on the creation of songs amid activities that combine words, voices, and physical movement.

2. The semantic and prosodic aspects of words as materials

Given that words as well as sounds are the materials of song-writing, this process has unique properties distinct from other forms of artistic construction activity. This is thought to derive from the semantic and prosodic aspects inherent in words.

Songs have words. Words have a semantic aspect in their content, intimately linked with human emotion, thought, intention, and so on. If the meaning of the words does not resonate, no one will want to sing them. Further, the prosodic aspect of the words — intonation, dynamics, tempo, timbre, etc. — provides a format to express inner emotions, thoughts, intentions, and so on externally. Since words are a tool for communication, when they are vocalized, they must follow the rules of speech. These rules include a prosodic aspect, that is, the unique pronunciation, rhythm, intonation and so on traditionally shared within the local society; when we speak our first language, we unconsciously speak in accordance with these rules. The prosodic aspect, related to these rules of spoken language, has generated the musical formats shared within the community.

Individual expression of emotion then takes place based on these shared musical

124

formats. Emotions reshape the elements of the prosodic aspect. The prosody of the words takes up a rhythm, creating unity and then repetition. The vowel sounds in the words may also be extended and vibrated. The inflection of the words is emphasized, with accents on specific syllables. The process in which spoken language thus takes shape is that of transforming speech, making it into song.

3. Cultural materials as "resistance" in song-writing

Because the words that act as the materials for song-writing are public, certain patterns in their chanting have been passed down through tradition. These patterns originate in the prosodic aspect of the words; for children living in Japan and speaking Japanese as their first language, the form has the deep familiarity of something heard in daily life. Scales, rhythms, and formats are elicited from the prosodic aspect of the words, and themselves elicit children's uncertain voice and give it form. Song-writing in Japanese may use the five-seven-five syllabic rhythm or the pentatonic scale of children's songs, developed from the prosodic aspect of Japanese. This rhythm and scale are familiar to the children, who have already encountered them somewhere in everyday life. When the children are made aware of modes they already have sensory familiarity with from everyday life, the song takes form.

Creating this awareness of modes may involve configuring them as "resistance." For example, the children might use a koto tuned to a major second intervals, the basic intonation of Japanese. Playing the "Daruma-san fell down" song, which has just two notes, on a koto with two strings will help them to confirm the pitch of the words and create songs using the scale of nursery rhymes.

The haiku five-seven-five syllabic rhythm, nursery rhymes, the koto, and so on are not only tools but also materials embodying the prosodic aspect of Japanese; thus, they constitute cultural materials. Through using cultural materials of this kind as "resistance," culture elicit impulse, and original ideas within culture become possible.

Instrument-making

Overview: instrument-making starts with the sounds that can be made from objects familiar to the children. In this activity, children work on familiar boxes, cans, water, bowls, and so on by striking, rubbing, or shaking them, exploring the sounds that result, and making music with the timbres and sound qualities thus created.

Instrument-making does not refer to producing existing instruments, such as making a flute out of bamboo. Children search for the sound they have in mind, while confirming the way each sound resonates. They then make the sound the arrive at into music through images. In the process of exploring the sounds of things ("what sound would this make?"), images such as "this sounds like the wind on a summer night" are formed, and the objects used to express these images come to function as instruments.

In this process of discovering the sound itself, various memories of qualities experienced in daily life are revived, becoming more easily perceived through images. Based on these images, the sound is constructed into music with a sense of harmony projecting a unified quality.

Stances

Instrument-making generally views instruments as the tools for making music. Based on this stance, the process is one of making replacement versions of existing model instruments. The instruments created are then used to perform existing pieces. For example, students might fill plastic bottles with rice to imitate maracas, using them to accompany a performance of "Twinkle Little Star." The point of deliberately making replacement instruments is to have children understand the mechanism of sound production in existing instruments and feel closer to them through production, providing motivation for performance.

However, there is also a stance that views instruments as materials for expression. This is the stance of instrument-making as artistic construction activity. In this context, the activity involves transforming outer materials (paper, boxes, bowls, cans, water, bamboo, etc.) and, in response to this transformation, recreating inner materials (images, thought, feelings, etc.). Therefore, the order is not "creating an instrument and then using it to express one's inner world," but expressing the inner world through working on materials, and through expression changing the materials once again, creating instruments through continuous interaction with the materials. The activity is not intended to produce instruments, but to make objects that are no more than materials into musical instruments.

Characteristics

1. Awakening of physical sensation in everyday life

Instrument-making is characterized by its pure concentration on the act of creating sound itself. This action involves the physical body along with vision and touch in addition to hearing. For example, the creation of a one-string box. This begins with taking a milk carton or similar box, putting a rubber band on it, and plucking the rubber band to make sounds. The children may then add notches to the milk carton, indent its edges, and so on in order to make sounds they like. These interactions with materials are done with the integration of the body and senses into a whole. When listening to the sound created, the children are not simply hearing its acoustics with their ears, but using their whole body to sense the sound, including the vibrations of the rubber band when plucked.

The children hear the sound emerging from the materials and imagine something. This process is entirely unlike that of a sound quiz, for instance, in which the teacher makes a sound in the classroom and asks the students to imagine what it sounds like. The quiz comes to an end when someone answers "It sounds like a festival," with no link to the next interaction. In artistic construction activity, however, children use all of their physical senses to sense and feel the sounds they have made. This process of sensing and feeling evokes the physical sensations of everyday life. The sound of water falling on the palm of the hand brings to mind moments of daily life when this occurred, in the bath or in the kitchen. When the physical sensations of daily life are brought to the children's attention, images are formed.

2. Imagination bringing meaning to sound

Instrument-making concentrates all physical sensations on the act of making sounds. Therefore, one of its advantages is that the act of searching for sounds and the formation of images are actively performed together. When children endow the sounds they have created with meaning through images, sounds and contexts familiar from everyday life emerge in rapid succession. Realizing that the sound of an empty can is "like sparkling water," children bring to mind memories of drinking sparkling water when younger, feeling that they could hear the bubbles. These memories involve the entire situation, not just the sounds. Experiences of qualities accompanied by feelings — the excitement of going out, the surprise of drinking sparkling water for the first time, the prettiness of its transparency — are all condensed into the image of "the sound of sparkling water bubbles."

Sensibility and imagination are significantly involved in image formation. Some children may listen to the sound of an empty can and think only "that just sounds like an empty can." This is because they are responding to the sound as a symbol. The ability to evoke an image of sparkling water of some kind, rather than responding to the sound as a symbol, is thought to depend on imagination. Instrument-making appears to be particularly effective in giving scope to — and thus leading to the cultivation of — sensibility and imagination.

Graphic score-making

Overview: Graphic score-making begins with an existing artwork (piece) of music by a composer. In this activity, while listening to a music piece, children cut colored-paper into shapes representing what they sense and feel from the music, and paste the shapes on large sheet of paper in correspondence with the construction of music piece. The final colored-paper diagram expresses the framework, construction, and images of the artwork. In this sense, the diagram is a kind of "graphic score" (See an example in graphic score produced by seven-year-old).

The act of cutting and pasting colored paper in itself is a form of play in which small children enjoy reshaping their materials. The act of cutting up paper is based on impulsion. Graphic score-making provides an objective for this kind of impulsive play.

Through the objective of making a graphic score matching the music, an interaction between the self and the music artwork occurs. The expressive medium here is the diagram. The diagram expresses externally the perceptions and feelings from the music artwork. Through this expression, the children listen to the music differently, reconstructing a new understanding and appreciation of the piece. Finally, the understanding and appreciation resulting from this reconstruction are expressed in a written critique. Graphic score-making is a learning activity in the area of appreciation, with the written critique as the "artwork."

Stances

School education takes two positions on graphic score-making. First is the stance seeing it as a compositional or creative activity. The graphic score itself appeared as a compositional method in contemporary music, using diagrams, symbols, and so on to express what could not be expressed in staff notation. The performance method is often left to the judgment of the performers based on the graphic score, and to happenstance. In school education, the method tends to be used as a performance activity (the teacher shows the children an existing graphic score and has them perform it based on their own free interpretations) or a compositional practice (the children write down their own pieces in graphic score form).

The other stance is that of graphic score-making as artistic construction activity. This method was developed as a learning method for music appreciation. In music appreciation activities, students are asked to perceive the framework of the music (how it is put together) and sense the qualitative characteristics it creates. These perceptions and feelings are to be connected and constructed overall as a written critique of the entire piece, expressing individual explanations and values.

Graphic score-making as artistic construction activity involves, as stated above, listening to a music piece and pasting diagrams of what was sensed and felt onto large sheet of paper, using colored paper to represent the construction of the music artwork. In short, this activity expresses what children sense and feel from music in graphic form. Graphic score-making connects the diagrams constructed outside the children with the perceptions and feelings about the music artwork constructed within them.

When the content of one's own perceptions and feelings is visualized as a diagram, it becomes possible to exchange that experience with others. Here the communication of qualities with others takes place, using the graphic score as the shared object. Through communication, new perspectives can be acquired, leading to new discoveries when applied to the original piece of music. In other words, this process enables a form of learning that reconstructs individuals' perspectives and ways of listening to the music.

Characteristics

1. Preconscious sensing of qualities

The activity of graphic score-making replaces the qualities mediated through music with those mediated through diagrams (colors and lines). Therein, the communication of qualities takes place within the group. When representing sensed musical qualities as a diagram, children cut and paste colored paper onto large sheet of paper without needing to explain themselves in words. Seeing one child in the group use yellow paper to represent a bright part in the music, another may add a little orange paper. By doing so, this child is conveying their sense of an orange-tinted warmth in the music, rather than the crisp yellow. This is the communication of qualities sensed from the music.

In this way, graphic score-making involves non-linguistic communication through diagrams, rather than communication through language. The identification of the qualities of the music takes place in the dimension before language — the preconscious dimension.

2. Conscious sensing of qualities

As stated above, language is not needed when creating diagrams. However, when asked by others why the colors and shapes of the completed diagram were chosen as they were, the explanation must employ language. In this situation, linguistic communication with others occurs. The preconscious sensing of qualities becomes conscious when put into words. As well, awareness arises of the formal aspects of music in the physical sense—rhythm, timbre, melody—which create these qualities. When these formal aspects are perceived, the identification of qualities as the content aspects of music likewise makes further progress. The more detailed the identification of qualities, the more abundant the meaning generated as a result within the interaction between the music and the self. An understanding of the piece that brings these together is obtained, enabling appreciation of the music as a whole.

In a case of music appreciation using St.-Saëns' "Aquarium" from *The Carnival of the Animals*, the class began with children expressing their sense of the music's qualities with general, conceptual words like "smooth." When asked about the basis for the diagrams by the teacher, however, they produced fragments of sensory, individual phrases like "wiggly," "dizzy," and "sparkling." Finally, they were able to endow the whole piece with meaning by telling it as a unified story through the connection of various sensed qualities via the process of graphic score-making. This transformation in linguistic expressions suggests that the qualities previously possessed unconsciously as preconscious experiences were identified and perceived consciously through the use of diagrams and language.

If vaguely sensed qualities constitute preconscious perceptions, graphic score-making brings them to conscious awareness by creating a space that raises questions about the diagram that would appear when representing these preconscious perceptions in colors and lines. Thus, the qualities of the music preconsciously sensed can be rendered conscious. The qualities of music sensed in appreciation activities can be converted from the dimension of preconscious perception to that of conscious perception through transformation into other qualitative media such as colors and lines.

3. Empathetic communication

The communication of qualities, particularly remarkable in graphic score-making, is notable for becoming empathetic communication, which creates an empathetic atmosphere in the class.

In the "Aquarium" case study above, the graphic scores were put on display in the classroom for other students to ask about. When someone asked "What's the second wave thing?" about Group A's diagram, Group A member T child answered "The strings made a wider sound the second time than the first, and got quieter the third time. Like a wave spreading and approaching the shore, and then sinking gradually back down." The class listened to the music, and children from other groups agreed "It's true, the second wave has this sense of approach!", while others supplemented the image: "The light blue dots at the beginning of the second wave are like splashes, I can get a sense of how the wave is approaching." The Group A children nodded in agreement as their classmates spoke. Here, others' interest in the qualities sensed created an empathetic atmosphere.

Graphic score-making is effective as a method of perceiving qualities in that it renders conscious qualities that are difficult to put into words, enabling concentration on the perception of qualities. Therefore, graphic score-making promotes the communication of qualities, strongly evoking interest in others when attempting to conjecture the qualities experienced by these others. This activity thus creates a situation in which empathetic communication is likely to occur.

NOTES

1. The practical examples are presented in detail in the following books.

Kojima, Ritsuko and Takahashi, Yoko, *Child's Sound World: education of freely making- music*, Reimei-shobo, Nagoya, 1995.

Kojima, Ritsuko, *Graphic Score-Making as Method of Music Appreciation*, Ongaku no tomo sha, Tokyo, 2011.

Kojima, Ritsuko and Kansai society for school music educational practice, *Education for Imagination by Musical Instrument-Making: theory and practice*, with documentary DVD video, Reimei-shobo, Nagoya, 2013.

Kojima, Ritsuko and Kansai society for school music educational practice, *Song Writing as Expression of Feelings in Daily Life: theory and practice*, with documentary DVD video, Reimei-shobo, Nagoya, 2014.

2. The writing score 2 is quoted from the following book. Kojima, Ritsuko, *Study on Child's Musical Development through Analysis of Construction Activity of School Music Classes*, Kazama-shobo, Tokyo, 1997, pp. 340-341.

An Example in Graphic Score

Writing Score2 : Blacksmith

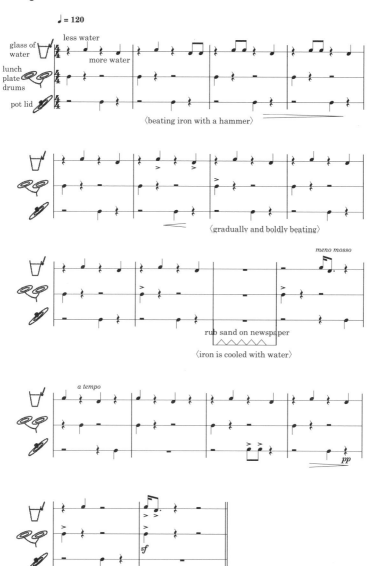

Conclusion
The Significance and Prospects of
Artistic Construction Activity

Part 1 of the conclusion will discuss the significance and challenges of the educational method of artistic construction activity in contemporary school education. Part 2 will address the future prospects of artistic construction activity in the 21st century, adopting the perspectives of the AI technological revolution and neuroscience.

Significance and challenges of artistic construction activity in school education

In Japanese school education, music classes generally use sheet music. Activities involve handing out sheet music to the students and having them convert the notes as symbols into sound, using voices or instruments. How is artistic construction activity different from traditional music classes of this kind? This section lists the characteristics of artistic construction activity and considers the significance and challenges of putting it into practice in school education.

Significance of artistic construction activity

1. Formation of the self via impulsion

First, artistic construction activity does not begin with music rendered into symbols, such as sheet music, but with children's inborn impulsion. Serving as the energy that furthers expression, impulsion realizes individuality when converted into desire or interest. That said, what is the significance of expressive activity focused on children's impulsion within school education?

Dewey argued that the source of emotion is need, as the impulsion of the organism (*LW*10: 21). The emotions accompanying impulsion are raw in nature. When impulsion attains expressive media and enters the indirect path of expression, instead of being discharged directly, impulsion is perceived as emotion. Like impulsion, emotion attains order and harmony through interaction with outer materials; finally, impulsion acquires order and harmony and becomes aesthetic emotion. Thus, when impulsion is led into the indirect channel of expression, the artwork is completed. A sense of fulfillment at having finished the job arises, and the initial raw emotion is ordered and made into aesthetic emotion (*LW*10: 83–85).

At the same time, impulsion and emotion are the sources of perception. Perception would never occur in the first place without the impulsion or desire to see things and hear sounds (*LW*10: 259–260). Impulsion does not disappear when entering the indirect channel of expression; rather, the desire arising from impulsion becomes attachment to the object, a conscious desire to see these things and hear these sounds. Expression involves the interaction of inner and outer materials. To bring the outer materials into the self, objects in the outer world are observed with conscious interest and attention. This is where perception occurs (*LW*10: 260). Without desire or attachment to the object, the simple reaction occurring would not result in perception. Impulsion is the source of emotion and, at the same time, the source of perception.

In this manner, expressive activities beginning with impulsion serve as self-expressive activities that engage the child's whole self, including emotion, perception, and will, as they attempt to fulfill their own desires. This is an experience in which the child becomes aware of the totality of life: "I am alive, here, now." The significance of expressive activities in school education with a focus on children's impulsion is the integration of emotion and perception education and the consequent formation of the self.

2. Development of imagination as an organ of perception of qualities

Activities in school music classes to date have had the existing world of art as their objective. By contrast, artistic construction activity enters the world of art in continuity with children's everyday life experience. Thus, children construct the sounds as materials into music, through interaction exploring sounds as materials using their bodies and senses rather than the mediation of symbols. This is the direct experience of sound. Given that artistic construction activity is centered on the direct experience of sound, a qualitative material, it provides abundant opportunities to experience qualities. The second characteristic of artistic construction activity is the experience of qualities. This signifies the development of imagination as an organ of perception of qualities.

Dewey considered "the world in which we immediately live" as "preeminently... qualitative" (LW5: 243), noting that "[a]ll direct experience is qualitative, and qualities are what make life experience itself directly precious" (LW10: 297). Qualities refer to the qualities of life experience, plentiful throughout life, rather than anything out of the ordinary. The existence of the qualities of life experience furthers our thought and action, serving as a foundation for the creation of science and art (LW5: 261). Dewey thus argued that "[t]hose who are called artists have for their subject-matter the qualities of things of direct experience" (LW10: 80) and that the essence of art is in clarifying and condensing meanings contained in scattered ways in the material of everyday experiences (LW10: 90).

However, qualities are essentially something to "be had" or to "be felt" (LW1: 198); we are not conscious of the qualities we experience in everyday life, which is to say they exist preconsciously, not yet recognized.

On the contrary, reflective experiences are derived within artistic construction activity. In reflective experiences, reflection brings the preconscious existence of qualities to the surface of consciousness. Qualities of past experience similar to the qualities being expressed in sound here and now are elicited, providing images that give meaning to the sound. That is, in artistic construction activity, children become aware through reflective experiences of the preconscious qualities of their own life experience, construct these qualities as meaning, and savor them. Artistic construction activity takes place as the experience of qualities.

Why is this experience important in education? Because it cultivates the imagination. The manipulation of materials in artistic construction activity relies on images. When the previously unconscious qualities of life experience are consciously perceived, they are given meaning by images. Imagination connects various images evoked by past life experience and composes them into an artwork with a grand unified vision. Imagination can also be called an organ of perception of qualities. Through the perception of the qualities permeating the situation of experience via imagination, phenomena and objects distant in time and space can be joined together. Therefore, imagination is not simply the ability to fantasize; it can be considered synonymous with the insight that perceives the invisible meanings of the world (Sloan: 139–190). Artistic construction activity, which calls for the work of imagination in qualitatively connecting and constructing various materials, contributes to the development of imagination.

3. Sense of reality through a foundation in life experience

The third characteristic of artistic construction activity is its foundation in life experience. Artistic construction activity does not involve being externally taught techniques and skills toward an existing model of expression and then creating artworks accordingly. Children rely on their own life experience when constructing sounds. With life experience in mind, they directly interact with sound to construct their artworks. What is the significance of the active evocation of life experience during artistic construction activity in the classroom? Children can acquire a sense of reality, of being alive here and now, through a foundation in their own life experience.

Artistic construction activity, which begins with everyday life experience, finds its component materials in everyday life. The tools used to create sound, the outer materials, are not instruments like the piano, which lack everyday familiarity, but materials with physical familiarity from daily life used as instruments. The inner materials of expression, as well, emphasize images from life experience.

Children have had various memorable experiences throughout their daily life. However, if left as is, even these experiences will remain no more than good memories. The meanings within their depths will not be realized. Thus, by engaging in artistic construction activity rooted in life experience at school, the children gain a new awareness of the qualitative meanings within the depths of their own experience.

These qualitative meanings are perceived in the form of images. For instance, a child might remember going to a New Year's festival and, amid the bustling crowd, hearing the sharp bang of the shooting gallery and seeing the bright colors of the fireworks. These pertain to the qualitative aspect of experience. When trying to express the New Year's festival, the children bring to mind the fascinating situations created by its various phenomena, which become images leading them into the activity.

Life experience grows broader in scope with each school year. For instance, older elementary schoolchildren might attempt to express outer space in sound. The train they remember riding is transformed into a spaceship, passes through a black hole, and encounters Halley's Comet, just as if they were expressing a real journey through outer space. All their previous experience of outer space is reconstructed, creating new images. Because these images are the unified, concentrated version of the children's own past experience, the use of sound to express the images is thought to convey a sense of definite reality.

Further, artistic construction activity involves, rather than the manipulation of symbols in the form of musical notation, the manipulation of materials that can be perceived by the senses. In short, this activity is one of direct experiences without the mediation of symbols. Here, the senses grasp the connection between means and end —how one's manipulation has changed the materials—as changes in qualities. This is an event in reality, not in the world of fantasy. Children are thus able to acquire a sense of reality: they are living in this world. For the increasing number of children who spend their time in the fantasy world of online gaming, artistic construction activity at school is significant in the valuable opportunity it provides for this sense of reality.

4. Creative communication through face-to-face interaction

The fourth characteristic is creative communication through face-to-face interaction. Artistic construction activity is a shared activity in which multiple children share the same purposes and images, not one performed by individuals in isolation. Therefore, each group creates one artwork. Although choral singing in traditional music classes can also be considered a shared activity, the fundamental difference between this practice and artistic construction activity is that in the latter, rather than focusing on a conductor, individuals create artworks through face-to-face communication with others.

One of the reasons why engagement with others is called for in artistic construction activity is that artistic expression activities require constant attention to the perspectives of others to avoid resulting in a self-absorbed product. Expression is a kind of communication. This is where the desire to create something that can be shared with society arises. As such, the artist must always be aware of the perspectives of others.

Another reason is that in order for the intellect to give direction to individual impulsion as exploratory activity, a space for face-to-face communication with others is required. Through communication with others, a common purpose is found; the group members exchange their expressive intents, images, concepts, and so on; and a single artwork is created in harmony. The word "construction" can be read with the nuance of connecting one's own possessions with those of others. When making these connections between the self and heterogeneous others, creativity arises. When opposing opinions or concepts arise in the practice of artistic construction activity, strangely enough, children often do not attempt to choose one or the other, but rather keep thinking about how both can be put to use.[1] Perhaps, the need to realize their own opinions or concepts enables them to conjecture that others feel just the same way. When trying to mediate the conflict, they often discover unexpected new techniques and images. Realizing that cooperation with others expands one's own world leads to putting cooperation into practice, not as some kind of moral rhetoric but as personal joy.

5. Formation of empathetic attitudes in the communication of quality

The fifth characteristic is that communication in artistic construction activity is the communication and, thus, the sharing of qualities. The messages being exchanged are the qualities that the self has experienced. Because qualities cannot be put into words, they are conveyed to others as images, using the qualitative media of sound, physical movement, color, shape, and so on. Here, non-linguistic communication takes place. Linguistic communication is used as an aid to its non-linguistic counterpart.

No one can convey their images to others exactly as they are; therefore, in the strictest sense, it is impossible to share the same images with others. For all a child may hear a friend murmur "It's like fine snowflakes softly falling" and empathize with the metaphor, their inner images are not the same. However, when multiple children share an activity in the same situation with a common purpose, they can share qualities such as the lightness and fluttering motion of the snow.

Precisely because qualities cannot be conveyed in words, the person hearing those murmured words concentrates on listening to the sound, trying to guess what the qualities behind the words sensed by the speaker are. The psychological action of trying to guess at what someone else has felt becomes the action of compassion toward them, leading to empathy. Conversely, empathy can occur precisely because qualities cannot be expressed in words, posing the need for the ability to perceive the qualities and images felt by the other person.

Empathy forms community. Community in artistic construction activity is different from the community created by conventional choral singing. It is not the affective sense of unity created by conformity, in the dimension of doing the same thing together. This community is created from shared qualities underpinned by the intellect, derived from the process of cooperative creation of an artwork, which involves problem-solving and inquiry.

Challenges

Artistic construction activity may be considered an archetype of human expressive behavior. The expressive behavior of selecting, ordering, and organizing sounds, an expressive medium, takes place in circulation between children's inner and outer worlds. This is an archetype of expression in that the manipulation of sounds takes place not abstractly in the mind but through repeated interactions between one's inner and outer worlds, using the hands to confirm the process of manipulation. Children who have acquired the archetype of expression through artistic construction activity are thought to become capable of expression in any type of media.

Considering artistic construction activity as an archetype of expression in this way, we come to the challenge of how to position this activity within the school curriculum, as occupation was positioned at the core of the Laboratory School curriculum. Questions arising here may include how children are to learn about human cultural heritage and how to make connections with learning experiences in other subjects. These two questions are discussed below.

1. Connection with cultural heritage, the outcome of humanity's artistic experience

Artistic construction activity is founded in children's life experience. To develop life experience continuously into artistic experience, artistic construction activity must consider and include culture and the arts in their role as the accumulation of human experience. However, we must note that this is not meant to render children's raw artwork more sophisticated. Therefore, the method adopted is not that of using widely accepted art as a model. This issue can be resolved through the concept that artistic construction activity is shared activity bringing together the self and others, who are different from the self. This viewpoint includes, among these "others," people in the distant past or in faraway lands. From this perspective, the elements of others' artistic experience can be connected to expand one's own.

One way to connect others' artistic experience with one's own, beyond time and place, lies in the form and content provided by the rhythms of nature. For instance, children's artistic construction activity often expresses the form of the "appearance and disappearance" of life provided by natural rhythms. These natural rhythms must have made their presence felt in human artistic experience all over the world and through the ages. Needless to say, they were likely expressed in the artistic experience of the artists who went down in history as well. Appreciating the artworks these artists produced from the perspective of the rhythms of nature leads to the expansion of the children's own artistic experience. The sensibilities of others raised through life experience in foreign lands express the universal rhythms of nature through different materials and in different forms. Having children interact with their products as an environment provides them with new concepts, giving rise to creativity. At the same time, the children also develop new ears, sensitive to new sounds. In this way, as they develop artistic experience by renewing the way they interact with sounds, they connect with others' artistic experience as a process of expanding their own. At the same time, this process ensures continuity from life experience to artistic experience.

Some of the challenges involved in enabling artistic construction activity to develop year by year, rather than remaining a temporary activity tethered to a given time in grade school, are how to construct the environment and how to include others' artistic experience as cultural heritage.

2. Development of artistic construction activity expanding artistic experience

This study has addressed artistic experiences in music as specific examples of artistic construction activity. However, artistic experience is not limited to music; it may also include visual arts, whose materials are colors and shapes, and dance, whose material is physical movement. Then there is drama, which unites multiple expressive media. While the expressive media may differ, the essence of artistic experience is the same "aesthetic experience as qualitative experience." Therefore, when developing specific artistic construction activities, the activity content may integrate and unite multiple expressive media. For example, in expression on the theme of the sea, individual differences may exist in the materials used to express the qualities of experiences of the sea. Having a wide variety of media available at this juncture may enable individuals to give full scope to their dominant sensibilities. Furthermore, in shared activity, one child's expression of images of the sea as a painting may stimulate new images or concepts in another child working on a musical expression with sound as their material. Through clarifying the principle here as artistic experience, it can become easier to conceive of activities integrating and uniting multiple arts, such as music, fine arts, and dance. Education, which offers a facile integration of the arts without keeping the principle of artistic experience in view, is likely to become ossified. The use of various expressive media connected on the basis of this principle is thought to be effective in developing, deepening, and expanding sensitivity.

Further, the integration and unity of artistic experience with other experience comes into view. The continuity of artistic experience with everyday life enables activities connected with the undifferentiated experience of everyday life as well. For instance, an activity may express the qualities experienced when growing morning glories in Living Environment Studies through sound, color, shape, or physical movement. This aids in the formation of the image to be expressed. As seen here, one challenge is the development of artistic construction activity that links artistic experience and other kinds of experience.

Prospects for artistic construction activity in the age of AI

As indicated in Part 1, artistic construction activity is a potential method for human development, beyond the scope of methods for music education. On this point, let us conclude with a view of the prospects for the significance of artistic construction activity in school education for human development, going forward in the 21st century. The 21st century may be considered the era of AI in a way never before experienced by humanity. The prospects for the significance of artistic construction activity in 21st-century school education are discussed here from two perspectives: the importance of the role of the arts education and their involvement in the qualitative world for the preservation of humanity in the age of AI and the importance of the role of direct experience for the evolution of the human brain, regardless of how technology may evolve.

Significance of arts education in the age of AI

As we enter the 21st century, we find ourselves facing an age of AI such as humanity has never experienced. In addition, we are forced to address the questions of what humanity is and what can be accomplished only by humans. Byron Reese, who documented the connection between technology and human history, predicted that the future of AI will be artificial general intelligence (AGI) approaching human capacity at another level from today's AIs (Reese: 2018). While AIs cannot teach themselves anything not in their program, an AGI would be able to update its own program. At this point, we must ask ourselves whether AGIs can be called human, and if not, what the difference is.

Reese's response to the question of what can be accomplished only by humans is "experience" of the world. AGIs lack the capacity for experience. Humans can sense the qualities of the real world through experience, possessed of consciousness. Consciousness has been described as the sense of happiness created by the smell of fresh bread or the pleasant scent of laundry just out of the dryer, that is, a sensation we experience in the first person. This sensation arises only in the real-life world of the natural environment, not in the digital world. No matter how many robots come to participate in society in the future, this experience of the qualities of the real world will be important for humans to retain their subjectivity. Dewey held that art concentrated and expressed the qualities thus experienced by humans and viewed this as its raison d'être.

This point confirms that the use of insight relying on uniquely human sensibilities in thought, and not only numbers will be important in controlling the direction of the future. For humans to remain human in the forthcoming era of AI, we will be called on to develop and cultivate our organs of perception of qualities through arts education. Here we find a basis for firmly positioning arts education within the school curriculum, not as hobby education but as education essential for human growth, on an equal footing with science education.

Significance of direct experience from a neuroscience perspective

As already stated, arts education is important in order for humans to remain human. However, methods matter when arts education is conducted in schools. The organs of perception of qualities will not develop through simply having children encounter artistic works, for instance, by forming choirs, giving violin lessons, or encouraging art appreciation. The method must be based on the raison d'être of the arts. This is where the artistic construction activity proposed in this study becomes meaningful.

The characteristics of artistic construction activity include direct experience. As noted above, artistic construction activity differs from conventional music education in its construction of music from sound, not through the symbols of sheet music but through direct interaction with sound. In recent years, developments in neuroscience have clarified how important direct experience is for brain formation. Koizumi Hideaki's *The Brain Develops Through Encounters: An Introduction to Neuroscience and Education* (2005) discusses this point as follows.

Neuroscience considers the basis of brain formation to be the body and the actual experience originating in the body. "Actual experience" here refers to direct experience. Why does neuroscience tell us that direct experience is important? First, the formation of the psyche is founded in the body. In direct experience, the physical senses are used to work directly upon the environment, without the mediation of symbols. According to Koizumi, humans reach out to and discover the outer world to live. That is, they create their outer worlds based on the body. The body is the foundation of the process through which humans attain consciousness and mind (Koizumi: 136).

Reaching out a hand to the outer world is both an act of impulse from the inside and an output to the outside. Reaching out a hand enables a variety of information to be input into the brain (Koizumi: 147). Babies grab things and put them in their mouths. They crawl from one spot to another. These actions input information into the brain. They confirm shapes, expand depth and breadth, and thereby create the individual's outer world. This leads to the development of vision and higher-order

association functions (Koizumi: 143–144). At the same time, the voluntary movements that accompany desires, such as crawling, are said to be related to emotional
neurotransmitters (Koizumi: 146). In short, the body serves as the foundation for the
creation of the human mind, emotion, and will.

Second, actual experience using the physical senses accumulates subconscious
information. Koizumi compared cognition to an iceberg. An iceberg has a part that
is visible above the water and a part that is submerged under the water. If the
visible part of the iceberg is the "conscious world," the invisible part is the "subconscious world" (Koizumi: 150). Our conscious awareness is just the tip of the iceberg,
compared with the contents of the subconscious. Subconscious information is input
through actual experience.

Koizumi mentioned that the subconscious world significantly influences human
cognition and behavior. For one, it is what renders abstract phenomena compre-
hensible (Koizumi: 150–151). To experience and understand the abstract, the
accumulation of actual experience is required. Further, information gleaned
through actual experience leads to behavior control as well as cognition. For instance, the experience of pain when cutting a finger enables the use of imagination
to predict this result, functioning as a real-life deterrent (Koizumi: 158).

Based on the above, the importance of direct experience from a neuroscience
perspective can be summarized as follows. Direct experience enables large amounts
of real-world information to be input into the brain at once; this information forms
the human subconscious. This subconscious accumulation of information enables
the realistic comprehension of the abstract, in addition to the imagination of the
whole from a part. This indeed is what Dewey meant by imagination. Given its
argument that the individual world expands with direct experience as its foundation, neuroscience can be said to have proved the significance of occupation and
artistic construction activity, which offer direct experience with raw materials.

The children of the future will grow up surrounded by artificial objects. In this
environment, artistic construction activity, involving direct interaction with natural materials such as sound, color, shape, and physical movement, will offer
plentiful opportunities to accumulate subconscious information based on the

trial-and-error nature of this interaction. Children will be able to accumulate the qualities of various experiences. It is hoped that this will help them to retain their selfhood while living in an artificial world.

Notes

1. Detailed examples of the practice of artistic construction activity from the perspective of resolving conflicting opinions can be found on pages 246–258 of Kojima, Ritsuko's *A Discussion of Children's Musical Development Through Analysis of Music Classes Centered on Construction Activity* (Kazama-shobo, 1997).

REFERENCES

In this book, all references to Dewey's writings are keyed to his Collected Works published by the Southern Illinois University Press. The abbreviations EW, MW, and LW, Followed by specific volume and page numbers, stand for Early Works, Middle Works, and Later Works within that series of publications.

Dewey, John. Plan of Organization of the University Primary School, 1895(?), *EW*5.

——. A Pedagogical Experiment, 1896, *EW*5.

——. The University Elementary School, 1898, *MW*1.

——. The School and Society, 1900, *MW*1.

——. The Place of Manual Training in the Elementary Course of Study, 1901, *MW*1.

——. Interest and Effort in Education, 1913, *MW*7.

——. Democracy and Education, 1916, *MW*9.

——. Experience and Nature, 1925, *LW*1.

——. The public and Its problem, 1926, *LW*2.

——. Qualitative Thought, 1930, *LW*5.

——. How We Think, 1933, *LW*8.

——. Art as Experience, 1934, *LW*10.

——.Logic: The Theory of Inquiry, 1938, *LW*12.

——. Experience and Education, 1938, *LW*13.

Jackson, Philip W. *John Dewey and the Lessons of Art*, Yale University Press, New Haven and London, 1998.

Kern, M. R. "Song Composition", Dewey, J. & Runyon L. (Eds.) T*he Elementary School Record: A Series of Nine Monographs*, No. 2, University of Chicago, 1900.

Koizumi, Hideaki. *The Brain Grows by Encounter: The Introduction to Brain Science and Education.* [Nou ha Deai de Sodatsu], 2005, Tokyo: Seito-sha.

Kojima, Ritsuko. *Study on Child's Musical Development through Analysis of Construction Activity of School Music Classes*, Kazama-shobo, Tokyo, 1997.

——. The Effectivity of "the Constructive occupation" as the Educational Method in "the integrated Learning", *Bulletin of John Dewey Society of Japan*, No. 42, 2001, pp.

174-179.

——. The Status of Warabweuta in School Education from the View point of "Constructive Activity": Continuous Transformation from Play to Study, *Bulletin of John Dewey Society of Japan*, No. 51, 2010, pp. 1-12.

——. *Graphic Score-Making as Method of Music Appreciation*, Ongaku no tomo sha, Tokyo, 2011.

Kojima, Ritsuko and Kansai Society for School Music Educational Practice. *Education of Warabeuta-Making in School: theory and practice*, Reimei-shobo, Nagoya, 2010.

——. *Education for Imagination by Musical Instrument-Making: theory and practice*, Reimei-shobo, Nagoya,2013.

——. *Song Writing as Expression of Feelings in Daily Life: theory and practice*, Reimei-shobo, Nagoya, 2014.

Mayhew, Katherine C. and Edwards, Anna C. *The Dewey School: The Laboratory School of the University of Chicago 1896-1903*, New Jersey: Aldine Transaction, 2007 (originally printed in 1936).

Mayhew, K. & Edwards, A. C. *The Dewey School: The Laboratory School of the University of Chicago*, 1896-1903, Aldine Transaction, New Jersey, 1965.

Mithen, Steve. *The Singing Neanderthals*, Phoenix, UK, 2006.

Shiraishi, Fumiko."Calvin Brainerd Cady: Thought and Feeling in the Study of Music", *Journal of Research in Music Education*, 1999, vol. 47, number 2, The National Association for Music Education: 150-162.

Sloan, Douglas. *Insight-Imagination: The Emancipation of Thought and the Modern World*, Green wood Press, Westport, CT, 1983.

Reese, Byron. *The Forth Age: Smart Robots, Conscious Computers, and the Future of Humanity*, Atria Books, New York, 2018.

ABOUT THE AUTHOR

KOJIMA Ritsuko, a specialist in music education and educational methodology, is an emeritus professor of Osaka Kyoiku University, Osaka, Japan. She received a bachelor's degree from Ochanomizu University, Tokyo, Japan, and a doctoral degree from Nagoya University, Nagoya, Japan. She has served as a representative of Japan Association for the Study of School Music Educational Practice, and an executive director of John Dewey Society of Japan. She was a member of the Conference for Course Guidelines of Music Education of the Ministry of Education, Culture, Sports, Science and Technology. Her books include *Artistic Construction Activity based on the Concept of J. Dewey's Occupation*, (with Sawada Atsuko) *Expression Education by Music: from inheritance to creation, Study on Child's Musical Development through Analysis of Construction Activity of School Music Classes*, and (with Takahashi Yoko) *Child's Sound World: education of freely making- music*.

著者略歴

小 島　律 子（こじま　りつこ）

大阪教育大学名誉教授・博士（教育学）（名古屋大学）。
専門分野　音楽教育学、教育方法学、教育実践学。
1950 年愛知県名古屋市生まれ。お茶の水女子大学文教育学部教育
学科（音楽教育学専攻）卒業、名古屋大学大学院教育学研究科博士
課程（教育方法学専攻）単位取得退学のち、大阪教育大学助手、講
師、助教授、教授を経て現在に至る。その間、文部科学省「中学校
学習指導要領（音楽）の改善に関する調査研究協力者」、日本学校
音楽実践学会代表理事、日本デューイ学会理事等を務める。
主な著書に、『構成活動を中心とした音楽授業の分析による児童の
音楽的発達の考察』風間書房、『音楽による表現の教育―継承から
創造へ―』（澤田篤子共著編）晃洋書房、『デューイのオキュペーシ
ョン概念に基づく芸術的構成活動』風間書房、等。

Arts Education Based on Dewey's Occupation:
Artistic Construction Activity

2023 年 11 月 1 日　第 1 刷発行　　　　　　　　　　・検印省略

著　者　　小 島 律 子

発行者　　木 村 慎 也

・定価はカバーに表示　　　　　印刷　中央印刷／製本　和光堂

発行所　株式会社　北 樹 出 版

〒153　東京都目黒区中目黒 1-2-6　電話(03)3715-1525(代表)